Serenade of Life Force
(Four Plays)

Serenade of Life Force
(Four Plays)
Prof. Sanghamitra Mishra

Translated by
Sanjeet Kumar Das

BLACK EAGLE BOOKS
Dublin, USA | Bhubaneswar, India

Black Eagle Books
USA address:
7464 Wisdom Lane
Dublin, OH 43016

India address:
E/312, Trident Galaxy, Kalinga Nagar,
Bhubaneswar-751003, Odisha, India

E-mail: info@blackeaglebooks.org
Website: www.blackeaglebooks.org

First International Edition Published by
Black Eagle Books, 2025

SERENADE OF LIFE FORCE (Four Plays)
by Prof. Sanghamitra Mishra

Translated by **Sanjeet Kumar Das**

Original Copyright © Prof. Sanghamitra Mishra
Translation Copyright © Sanjeet Kumar Das

All rights reserved. No part of this publication may be reproduced, stored in a retrieval system, or transmitted, in any form or by any means, electronic, mechanical, photocopying, recording or otherwise without the prior permission of the publisher.

Cover & Interior Design: Ezy's Publication

ISBN- 978-1-64560-675-8 (Paperback)

Printed in the United States of America

Author's View

For any auspicious work, time is already scheduled beforehand. It is proven in my life, time and again. This work of art comprises four of my plays translated into English with the title *Serenade of Life Force*. It gives me immense pleasure. My plays are not theoretically based but very realistic. I have penned down these plays the way I have observed 'time and society' and wanted to see them. I have chosen the characters roaming in my surroundings for my plays. The talent and brilliance of women in society can build the golden bridges in relationships among people. Here, characters like Sinu and Giti can work as the wealth and pride of the families; Suchana is not only a name 'Suchana' but an officer who can provide information to the public on different domains of human life and in the 'Last Quarter of Anticipation' the women especially Parbati, will even see the brighter side of life. I appeal to society to have faith in women for a better tomorrow.

On his own choice, Sanjeet Kumar Das, an Assistant Professor Department of English, Central University of Odisha, has earnestly translated my plays "Subarna Setu" as "Golden Bridge", "Pratikshara Antima Prahar" as "Last Quarter of Anticipation", "Ama Giti Ama Sanskruti" as "Our Giti: Our Pride", and "Suchana Gotie Jhiara Naan" as "Suchana: The Name of a Girl" respectively. It shows his love for language, strong avidity in plays, and tremendous enthusiasm to render our Odia language and literature a global platform for a broader readership. The translation is a co-creative work. It's like nurturing someone else's child as one's own and helping the child grow in the best possible manner and is well-established in society. I am thankful to him for having a good grasp of my plays and translating them into English.

Through these four plays, I hope, though not holistic but partial lifestyle of Odias, to reach the people of different countries and continents and the Odia (immigrants) who are permanently settled abroad.

I am grateful to the director of Black Eagle Books, Sri Satya Patnaik, and his associate, Sri Ashok Parida, for their kind gesture to publish my plays as a work. I would also like to thank my student, Dr. Pradosh Kumar Swain, an Assistant Professor at the Department of Odia, Central University of Odisha, Koraput, for establishing the link between me and Sanjeet Babu and for his interest in my works being translated.

Prof. (Dr) Sanghamitra Mishra

Translator's View

Prof. (Dr) Sanghamitra Mishra is an acclaimed critic and writer who has earned her name in Odia language and literature. Here, I have attempted to translate her four short Odia plays into English as "Golden Bridge", "Our Geeti: Our Pride", "Suchana: The Name of a Girl", and "Last Quarter of Anticipation" respectively, and rendered the title *Serenade of Life Force* for this collection of plays for the readers to go through on the global platform. In all the plays, female characters are vibrant. They act as connecting links to bridge the gap perceived in human relationships in society. All the domestic plays are with characters chosen from real-life situations. The follies and foibles of human life are with ups and downs strewn nicely together but never thwarted permanently because of the life force already within every individual and consistently reinforces them to move upward. This life force galvanizes the characters taken into consideration in all the plays concerned herewith the female protagonists to fight against the social oddities and stereotypes sometimes silently, but often to socialize, negotiate, and poise with society convincingly. The dramatist has played a masterstroke in bringing these characters to the limelight and proving that their active participation in families and societies practically reduces the tension erupting anywhere.

I have marked the female characters in all the plays cited here as striving hard to prove and celebrate what they have been naturally endowed with. They have showcased their talent, though they get hiccoughed sometimes for the generation gap, and social stereotypes, and receive a huge round of applause later for their bravery to nourish their inborn talent. The playwright motivates the girls, ladies, and older women to acclimatize and conform themselves to contextual socio-cultural practices and advocates to lead society with the talent they are with. By doing so, they can manifest their identity and recognition. She advertises that they should be with the system, understand it better, and indulge in social discourses completely, following the 'Principle of Togetherness' for any changes if their society lags. For a healthy society, the role of women is crucial and can't be denied. Women are instrumental in restoring moral values in society and are fast and sensible to the socio-cultural changes the world is moving on. The characters like Sinu in the play "Golden Bridge", Geeti in the play "Our Geeti: Our Pride", Suchana in "Suchana: The Name of a Girl", and Parbati in "Last Quarter in Anticipation" are here to represent different categories of women in society. All the women subjugated in the social system neither revolt strongly nor imitate wholly and passively. They try to understand and judge the matter for their contextual priority and ascertain their role with closer approximation and vitality. This is what the uniqueness of the playwright is for the rest to practise.

This discussion reminds me of one of the leading prominent critics of the contemporary period, Elaine Showalter's critical essay "Towards a Feminist Poetics," wherein three different phases, the 'Feminine Phase', 'Feminist Phase', and 'Female Phase', are considered. Prof. Sanghamitra Mishra can be categorized into the third 'Female Phase' as a playwright. She perceives and celebrates women's strength as being bold and having the patience to understand others in family and society and act accordingly.

I have tried my best to keep the language as lucid as possible. I came across some natural shifts while following the 'principle of equivalence' and the 'principle of faithfulness' between the Odia language and the English language. The culture-specific terms of the source language texts are maintained as they are.

I earnestly thank Professor Sanghamitra Mishra for believing me to translate her texts carefully. A renowned professor of Odia Literature, she retired from Utkal University. I convey my heartfelt gratitude to Dr. Pradosh Kumar Swain, Assistant Professor, Department of Odia Language and Literature, Central University of Odisha, for helping me select her texts for my work.

Finally, I sincerely thank my students of M. A. in English Programme, Central University of Odisha, like Padmalaya Thatoi for "Golden Bridge", Anjali Patra for "Last Quarter of Anticipation", and "Suchana: The Name of a Girl" and Prateek Patnaik for "Our Geeti: Our Pride" for submitting me their initial drafts.

I convey my heartfelt gratitude to Sri Satya Pattanaik, the director of Black Eagle Books, USA, and Sri Ashok Parida of the publishing house for their kind consent to publish the text in time.

Sanjeet Kumar Das

CONTENTS

Golden Bridge	13-43
Our Geeti: Our Pride	45-65
Suchana: The Name of a Girl	67-88
Last Quarter of Anticipation	89-132

Golden Bridge

Dramatis Personae

Kishore Babu	:	An old man having faith in Gandhism
Sunayana	:	Wife of Kishore Babu
Sinu	:	Daughter of Kishore Babu and Sunayana Devi, later wife of Badal
Sudhir Babu	:	A respectable person in a middle-class family
Leeli Devi	:	Wife of Sudhir Babu
Badal	:	Son of Sudhir Babu
Chhanda	:	Daughter of Sudhir Babu and Leeli Devi
Chandan	:	Lover of Chhanda

SCENE- I

[It's 6.30 am. Kishore Babu is reading the newspaper. His better half, Sunayana, enters holding a tea tray. Putting that tray on the teapot, she touches his feet.]

Kishore Babu : Why did you touch my feet in the morning? Is it *Savitri Amavasya* today? (Taking off his reading glasses) Why can't I hear the chanting of mantras to the deity? Why haven't you dressed in a new saree?

Sunayana	:	You are great! Today is our marriage anniversary. Can't you remember? - I knew you would forget this.
Kishore Babu	:	Oh, my goodness! I have forgotten it. How many years have we been together? (Counting) Yes, perhaps it's the thirty-fifth year – Am I right?
Sunayana	:	Yes, if you count wrongly, there won't be any problem. As if I am always a sweet sixteen. Please, have tea. I still remember how much sugar is to be added.
Kishore Babu	:	Today you look so gorgeous… but
Sunayana	:	But what? I have grey hair- I wear glasses.
Kishore Babu	:	Not that, if you get a chance, you will sling the arrows of words.
Sunayana	:	Leave it. Slinging many arrows, I have become an older woman. You have come to this earth with impregnable armour.
Kishore Babu	:	You are right. Do you know how grateful I have been to my parents? They have chosen a woman like you to be my wife. And I- leave that old story.
Sunayana	:	It would have been better if a girl of your choice had come. You would know how you were forgetting everything.
Kishore Babu	:	Past is passed. Now you say how we will celebrate it today.
Sunayana	:	What celebration? We may receive one phone call or an SMS within half an hour—Happy Marriage Anniversary…. or of this kind.
Kishore Babu	:	Yes, but our children remember this well.
Sunayana	:	That's also right. Something is better than

	nothing. It's better to see in one eye than never seeing anything.
Kishore Babu :	Nina, I understand your self-esteem, but-
Sunayana :	Do you remember? When they were kids, sometimes they offered us chocolates, and sometimes handed over the bouquet of wildflowers plucking from the garden to us on our marriage anniversary. I recall, one year, they both saved money and brought a pair of sleepers for you and a piece of cloth to stitch a blouse for me.
Kishore Babu :	Yes, I have remembered all that. And later, growing up, they insisted on us having food in the hotel. They were citing examples of their friends. I have also thrown parties many times in the hotel.
Sunayana :	Nobody is here now with us. They are busy with their families. They don't have time to think about their parents.
Kishore Babu :	When man attains adulthood, his priority changes. When Bubu and Sinu were studying, you could recall how we sat for hours beside them. You have denied attending any marriage party and sacred thread ceremony or even going for marketing for those days.
Sunayana :	Yes, when I visited my in-law's house for eight-ten days during vacation, I would take on my responsibilities. Not only that there. I send something to my parents and siblings on the eve of *the Raja* festival every year.

Kishore Babu	:	That was your nature- Generosity and sacrifice for both the households.
Sunayana	:	It's neither nature nor generosity, but purely a sense of guilt. This was exhaustion or languor, as we only sometimes stayed with them. But these children do not have that exhaustion or guilt either.
Kishore Babu	:	They are children of this age. Leave that, don't recollect all that, and say what we will do today.
Sunayana	:	What will we do? I will cook as I usually do like other days. You will get by heart the newspapers or talk to somebody over the phone.
Kishore Babu	:	You have started again?
Sunayana	:	How can I start when you have yet to finish? If there is no disruption of the power supply in this suburb, switching on the T.V. will cause you to be absorbed in deep concentration. Then, the entire day will pass vaguely.
Kishore Babu	:	Hey, all these are cancelled today. Finish your work. Let's visit the temple.
Sunayana	:	(Arranging the cup and saucer/ plate on the tray, she enters the kitchen.)
Kishore Babu	:	(To himself) How come we have spent so many days? It's the same type of monotonous work! That life! What Nina understands is final – oh, no- who will help her understand those pages of the book have been turned over? (The phone rings.)

Kishore Babu	:	Hello… yes… I will tell your mom… she is in the kitchen. When? Okay, all right… you are busy, okay… bye…bye. (He disconnected the call.) (To himself) If you don't have time, what's the need to call us? When we have not pointed out your principal faults, how could we say that you have made a mistake not wishing us over the phone? Nina… Nina… (Calling) (Sunayana comes from the kitchen.)
Sunayana	:	Why are you calling me loudly?
Kishore Babu	:	Oh, your dear darling son Bubu rang you?
Sunayana	:	Why didn't you give me the phone?
Kishore Babu	:	He said, "He does not have time." He rang us only to wish. He will talk to you later. Is it okay?
Sunayana	:	You know that time will come after two months. That's my fate. Why are you calling me after disconnecting the phone? A call, a howling call is regularly heard, as if somewhere a house was burning!
Kishore Babu	:	(smiling) You must update the term you used here. Neither is there any thatched house, nor is anybody calling while a home is set on fire.
Sunayana	:	Let this be used until we breathe last. (leaving)
Kishore Babu	:	(Again to himself) Marriage Anniversary', 'Valentine's Day'- From where have these dates come from to our culture? These are only showy nature. Oh, nobody announces love by beating drums. No

need to comment on this matter. (He sings an old Odia movie song tracing from his memory.)
My eyes' many words,
My mind's silence
I want to say but can't,
Without saying, I can't stay.
(He murmurs silently. Sunayana comes in.)

Sunayana : This time, breakfast tea is in your hand.
Kishore Babu : Wah Sunayana, what an arrangement! My favourite *Kobipakudi* (marinated cauliflower fry)! Vah, mouthwatering snacks!
Sunayana : Have less of this snack carefully. When there was the want, you had less quantity after serving our children. Nowadays, you are not well. Cholesterol rises. I prepared this item because it is easily made. You won't have all this. You will keep that for me. (She leaves.)
Kishore Babu : Please, come. Today, let's have it together. I am waiting for you.

SCENE- II

[Both sit after having had lunch. The doorbell rings. Sunayana opens the door. A girl coming inside touches her feet. Sunayana looks at her, surprised.]

Chhanda : Aunt, I am Chhanda. You can't recognize me. [Touching Kishore Babu's feet in respect.]
Kishore Babu : Very nice that you have come to our home. Who else is with you?

Sunayana	:	Leave that. What would you like to have, my dear? We have just had our lunch. Come with me and have what we are with.
Kishore Babu	:	Bring here what we have. Sit here, Chhanda – Let your aunt come – [Sunayana leaves.]
Chhanda	:	Uncle, I guess you have some queries. I have come here because I couldn't find any other way out. My sister-in-law says you can solve all the problems.
Kishore Babu	:	Sinu has told me this. Let me know your problem first. Let us respect her words. When she is your sister-in-law…
Chhanda	:	What's the story? Oh, yes, my dad has fixed the marriage.
Kishore Babu	:	The excellent news. Your dad is a considerate man. Where's the problem?
Chhanda	:	Uncle, how can I say you? That boy calls me over the phone to gossip with him and go on a trip. [Sunayana enters with a food plate.]
Sunayana	:	Who calls whom?
Kishore Babu	:	Please be seated. Let Chhanda finish her story. Yes, speak, my dear.
Chhanda	:	I denied it. I told him about our family tradition. Do you know what he said to me? He said, "I am very proud and stubborn." The girls are waiting in queue to gossip with him. There are many points like this.
Sunayana	:	Oh, it's the matter. Nowadays, boys and girls are roaming in pairs. It would be

		best if you had wandered with him. Our times were different.
Kishore Babu	:	Don't play on the old recordings. (To Chhanda) What do you think about this? Let me hear from you first.
Chhanda	:	I have already expressed my views, uncle. Had I known this before, it would have been different. Why will I wander with him? My sister-in-law has also told me to invite him to our home and have a word with him.
Kishore Babu	:	It's good. My daughter has already suggested this step before I tell you.
Chhanda	:	Please, say. If many girls agree to talk and roam with him, what's the need for him to marry me?
Sunayana	:	Hey, he must be fickle-minded and modern.
Kishore Babu	:	And our Chhanda is an old-fashioned and outdated girl. Hold on- we will hear from her. Have you told your parents about this?
Chhanda	:	My mom says no boy is blamed for this. People don't find faults with boys.
Sunayana	:	What does your dad say?
Chhanda	:	My dad says this is very common nowadays. If we reject this proposal, is there any guarantee that we will get a good boy for our daughter's marriage?
Kishore Babu	:	Then, what does your father want?
Chhanda	:	Both dad and mom say, if you reject the proposal, we won't search for any bridegroom for you. Do what you

	want- if you marry, it's good. If not, no problem.
Sunayana :	When sons and daughters are home, proposals come from different places. It's not good to deny the relationship.
Kishore Babu :	Hello, my dear. Do your parents know that you came here?
Chhanda :	No, Uncle, only my sister-in-law knows that I have come here. I must return home by evening.
Sunayana :	Give a call to your home. Stay here tonight. Today is our marriage anniversary.
Kishore Babu :	Nina, you don't understand the importance of the matter. You think of only marriage anniversaries and feasts.
Sunayana :	Okay, now she has come to our home. She has not gone to someone else's house! It's her sister-in-law's maternal place.
Chhanda :	No, Aunt, by evening, I must be home. I told my parents I was going to my friend's house. Yes, aunt, I have been absorbed in my issue. How old is your marriage now? [She touches their feet.]
Kishore Babu :	Okay, my dear – perhaps this is our thirty-fifth year.
Chhanda :	My sister-in-law must have known this! She may be forgetting this in her children's issues.
Sunayana :	This was not celebrated in our time. Then our marriages were held either four days before *Rathaytra* (Car Festival of Lord Jagannatha) or two days after *Agirapurnami* (fire festival held on the full

		moon day of Magha) or sometimes on the day of Saraswati Puja celebration. It passed on like this.
Kishore Babu	:	What have you decided, my daughter?
Chhanda	:	I have decided to refuse or deny him.
Sunayana	:	You are highly educated. You will get a job tomorrow. Why can't you choose someone of your choice?
Chhanda	:	The same thing happens there, too, Aunt; my dad will ask whether his parents have a flat in the city or whether the boy has brothers and sisters. Love starts after knowing all this.
Sunayana	:	And the girls? What do they enquire?
Chhanda	:	Apart from this, they will ask whether he has a bike or a car. How much will he spend on their entertainment? Whether his parents are old-fashioned or not?
Kishore Babu	:	It's a matter of business, my dear. How much will you benefit from spending a certain amount?
Sunayana	:	What do you say? Love is blind. Caste doesn't matter in love. Then what profit or loss?
Chhanda	:	Aunt, those love stories are in the novels. Everything is calculated here. Is there any guarantee that the person whom I choose will understand me well?
Sunayana	:	Don't proceed with these thoughts ahead, my dear. You see, we have been staying together with our strengths and weaknesses. Your uncle may only like some of my suggestions, or I don't accept

		all his decisions, but the family runs with some negotiations.
Kishore Babu	:	Stop your mouth. I say, 'Take two more years in the name of research.' Convince your parents. You appear in competitive examinations during this period. If you get through, you will stand on your own. You will solve your problem.
Chhanda	:	What shall I do now? Having seen my dad, I get annoyed, and I am also bruised. Please don't talk to my mother. My elder brother is also silent. Yes, he is the most eligible son. He will never go against my parents' words.
Sunayana	:	Is our Sinu well?
Chhanda	:	Yes, my sister-in-law is all along with me. She is my friend, well-wisher, and with her ideas and permission I have reached here. It's a great day for me. I have joined you. I am fortunate. Now I am leaving.
Kishore Babu	:	You will ring us, my dear- you will also tell Sinu to give us a call.
Sunayana	:	Both will try to adjust and convince each other. You will see your problems are getting solved.
Chhanda	:	Aunt. I will obey your words. I am leaving, then… (She leaves.)

SCENE- III

[It's Sinu's in-law's house. Sinu and Badal are talking to each other.]

Sinu : You can have a word with our dad. It's not tough at all. Your sisters' fate depends on it.

Badal : What do you say? I can't say anything. Do you have any ideas about our family?

Sinu : It has already been seven years since I came here. Dad and Mom are not so obstinate that they will insist when you ask them.

Badal : Oh, no. You think of her family. Dad will say, "You search for her bridegroom's house." I can't step into the problem.

Sinu : Tomorrow, our daughter will be like Sinu. Then, won't you say so?

Badal : It's your nature to extend the conversation. She is their daughter. They will do what they want.

Sinu : She is their daughter. Isn't she anything to you? [Chhanda comes in.]

Chhanda : Yes, *Bhauja* (sister-in-law), my elder brother, is very educated. He earns a lot.

Badal : Don't interfere in our discussion, Chhanda.

Chhanda : Can you beat me? What's new in it, *Bhai* (Brother)? My mom says, twisting my ear; you have brought it to this condition. Listen to me: your marriage proposals came from different places, but I rejected most of them for not being up to your choice. You have often told me, "Chhanda, I don't like the proposal.

		Please do something to reject." I solved the problems in my way.
Badal	:	It's okay, but-
Chhanda	:	Today, it's your turn, Bhai. Otherwise, I will believe in my destiny. Both man and God are very cruel to me. [She leaves.]
Sinu	:	You see, the stubbornness of the younger one – Can we not search for anyone suitable to marry Chhanda except Mohan or Manidra?
Badal	:	Let me try. (While going) Sinu, you know my friend Sulata – I met her today. She is not staying with her husband. Perhaps they are going to be separated.
Sinu	:	Oh, that Sulata who attended my marriage party with her toy-like daughter. Her daughter must be in her early teens.
Badal	:	She may be nine to ten years old. What will Sulata do?
Sinu	:	The one who told you she would be separated from her husband must have thought of doing something.
Badal	:	She looked fresh and said, "I was stirred in hell for many days and no more." She seems to be courageous now.
Sinu	:	Yes, but until today, society recognizes the girl as the 'Best Daughter/ Woman' who has suffered a lot. One who leaves hell or hell leaves that one, maybe the master of all attributes, won't be accepted either by society or the family.
Badal	:	Stop your lecture. (Chhanda enters.) Where has my mom gone?

Chhanda	:	*Bhauja* (Sister-in-law), I want to tell you something. Please come with me. (whispering)
Chhanda	:	(entering) Where's the mobile? Please give me it for a second.
Badal	:	Are you reminded of?
Sinu	:	Running after the kids, I forget everything. Today is my parents' marriage anniversary. It's now the dread hour of the night.
Badal	:	How did Chhanda know about your parents' marriage anniversary?
Sinu	:	Not that. She was telling me something else. You should not know this.
Badal	:	It's okay. I am tapping the number; you can talk – (pressing the numbers) Hello, Dad, happy marriage anniversary! Please hold for a second; Sinu will speak to you.
Sinu	:	Daddy, my entire day is spent. I was swamped. How did you celebrate this day? Okay, I will call you later. Children are shouting there. You will pass the message to Mom.
Badal	:	Sinu, what do you say? I will tell my dad to reject this marriage proposal.
Sinu	:	Please try once. If you say, Mom will stand by you. (To herself for a while) How can the boys become so indifferent? I have come from another family. I am worried for Chhanda. (Chhanda enters.)
Chhanda	:	*Bhauja*, switch on the T. V for news. Let us watch- forget this superfluous matter. Marriages are held in heaven. I have not

		come to this world for him. Let them beat their heads or whatever they may say to me. (Watching the news- after a while)
Chhanda	:	*Bhauja*, listen to the news carefully. News speaks about your Mahendra or Manish?
Sinu	:	Nowadays, you will hear the name of Manish only in every name.
Chhanda	:	Hear (Youth arrested for taking lakhs of rupees from unemployed young boys and girls and assuring them the jobs.) His name is Manish Nayak. Police are searching for his associates now.
Sinu	:	He may be somebody else. Switch off the T.V.
Chhanda	:	He is nobody else, Bhauja. He is the highly qualified bridegroom my dad has chosen for me and is the one about to go abroad shortly. Thanks God. My life is saved.
Sinu	:	Let's have dinner. (Badal enters.)
Badal	:	Hey, Sinu! You see why your dad rings us late at night. How is he?
Sinu	:	Daddy, what happened? News… Yes… No. I will call you tomorrow. Bye.
Badal	:	What news?
Sinu	:	We are yet to watch the news dad watched. We will watch it at 11.00 pm.
Badal	:	Who will wait till 11.00 pm? We will watch it tomorrow morning. Let's have dinner. (He leaves.)
Chhanda	:	Oh, you have relieved me, *Bhauja*.
Sinu	:	My mom says, "No one is considered

		guilty if one saves someone's life by telling pardonable lies."
Chhanda	:	Frankly speaking, my uncle and aunt are great and blessed for their worthy daughter like you.
Sinu	:	Let's go, or else others can think our discussion will continue.

SCENE- IV

[Next day morning. Sudhir Babu reads the newspaper. He is Badal's father.]

Sudhir Babu	:	Hey, Badal and Sinu, come here immediately. See the newspaper here.
Badal	:	What's dad?
Sudhir	:	Read the news here. This Manish is a fraud.
Sinu	:	(Coming quickly) Who's a fraud, Dad?
Sudhir	:	Our Manish. The man with whom I decided to do Chhanda's marriage.
Sinu	:	How did he become our Manish? Chhanda didn't show any interest in him. It's good that the disease has not affected our family.
Badal	:	Dad, we would have finished the 'Ring Ceremony'?
Sudhir	:	You are talking about the ring ceremony. They were insisting on finishing the marriage. If I had finished Chhanda's marriage? My destiny -
Sinu	:	Dad, Thinking and consulting others, one should do a daughter's marriage. You are...
Badal	:	Sinu, don't say this to our dad.

Sinu	:	Dad, you are our superior, guardian. You are Chhanda's dad. How much would you have been hurt if you had done this marriage? Besides, Mom has gone to her father's house for eight days.
Sudhir	:	Boys in today's world…
Badal	:	Since the day he dated our Chhanda and requested a trip, I felt very awkward.
Sudhir	:	Why didn't you tell me?
Badal	:	Dad
Sinu	:	Dad, I have often told him to open his mouth. Don't spoil your daughter's life.
Sudhir	:	Did you know this, my daughter?
Sinu	:	No, Dad, but when he said to finish the marriage soon and to hand over the cash for dowry to them, I felt terrible. After calling Chhanda, he said, "Girls run after me." I disliked that man that day only-honestly speaking.
Sudhir	:	But none of you told me. I was sticking to what I understood. Our Chhanda is lucky. Today, this word…
Sinu	:	Dad, if I had told you this, you wouldn't have believed me.
Badal	:	Leave it. It's better not to have any further discussion about the matter. Nowadays, most terrible incidents are happening.
Sudhir	:	Yes, you are right. Dowry was a significant issue in the past. Murdering and branding with a heated piece of iron has become a common practice in today's world.
Badal	:	Dad, how can I explain to you the most dangerous incidents than that?

Sudhir	:	What's the matter you can't tell your father?
Badal	:	Nowadays, the lover and beloved's nude portraits are uploaded online. Very heinous crime...
Sinu	:	(To Badal) Dad shouldn't know that. He will be worried unnecessarily.
Sudhir	:	Social media like Facebook, the internet and Google have ruined our society and culture.
Badal	:	Dad, how did you know all this? I think.
Sudhir	:	Oh, I am reading newspapers and watching television. Can't I know this much? [Leeli Devi reaches there.]
Sudhir	:	Hey, Sinu! Your mother-in-law has arrived here.
Leeli	:	I have heard you here for the last five minutes. Frankly saying, you were intelligent in your time, but today, you are unfit and a fool.
Badal	:	Mom, you started quarreling as soon as you reached here. How did you stop your mouth for the last eight days?
Sinu	:	I had read a story that the mother of one son and daughter, a housewife, talking over the internet for hours, had given up her home.
Sudhir	:	What's that story?
Leeli	:	How will you know that? That's beyond your understanding. I have heard about the man who was chosen for Chhanda...
Badal	:	Mom, we have saved Chhanda's life. Let our Chhanda be with us – She has

		not ruined her life plunging into hell. (Chhanda enters.)
Chhanda	:	Since you have left the place, we have been facing problem after problem. Oh, Mom, my luck has favoured me.
Leeli	:	Yes, my dear, not only yours but also ours.
Leeli	:	All right, tomorrow your dad will go for a cardiac checkup. Recalling this I rushed, otherwise I would have stayed there for three to four more days. Do you people remember that or not.
Sinu	:	You have not called us at all. We missed you a lot.
Leeli	:	There is a power cut for half a day. That nephew has a mobile phone. He keeps that one in his pocket day and night. I couldn't sense the time spent gossiping with your aunt.
Badal	:	Having reached here at the right moment, you have reminded us of my dad's checkup. It's nice. We will all go to Cuttack. While returning, we will visit Sinu's house.
Sudhir	:	You are right, my dear. Since I have fallen sick, Sinu has forgotten her father's house. Having seen us, they will also be happy.
Sinu	:	Dad, I am lucky.
Leeli	:	Why are you only lucky? We are fortunate, too, for you are our daughter-in-law.
Sudhir	:	Okay. Do your preparation today. Tomorrow morning, we have to be ready.

Sinu	:	Dad, let me check whether Ladli's (daughter's) sir has gone.
Leeli	:	Let's go (calling Chhanda). Where are you, Chhanda?
Chhanda	:	(Entering) It's good that you have come, otherwise...
Leeli	:	Or else what? How could your father have fixed your marriage without asking me? Can he dare to do so?
Sudhir	:	It's okay; this is all my mistake. Stop your mouth now.

SCENE- V

[Kishore Babu's apartment. The calling bell rings.]

Kishore Babu	:	(Opening the door) Wonderful! How fortunate we are today! We met our relatives. Hey Nina, come here. See who has come.
Sudhir Babu & Leeli Devi	:	Namaskar! (Badal and Sinu touched the feet.)
Chhanda	:	Namaskar, Uncle and Aunt!
Kishore Babu	:	Stay blessed! God bless you!
Sinu	:	Dad, I haven't seen you both for many days.
Sunayana	:	Oh, my dear! We are at a far-off place. Your father-in-law and mother-in-law are also your parents here!
Badal	:	We came to Cuttack for our dad's checkup. Dad told me to return this way. We will give a surprise to your father-in-law and mother-in-law.

Kishore Babu	:	Oh, Nina! Take care of Sinu's father-in-law and mother-in-law. Don't gossip only.
Sunayana	:	Well, Chhanda, that day at the right time…
Chhanda	:	Aunt, please come; I will help you in the kitchen.
Kishore Babu	:	Yes, you go. One inherits traits from the family occupation. Charity begins at home. Other than Chhanda, who else can understand this?
Badal	:	Let me visit the market for a while. By evening, we will start our journey.
Leelidevi	:	You can stay at your father-in-law's house for three to four days. We are accompanying our daughter-in-law.
Kishore Babu	:	What you say, *samuduni*…
Sunayana	:	Then I am coming. You gossip. (after a while)
Badal	:	Oh, the strike is on the road. How will we go?
Leelidevi	:	Why? What happened?
Badal	:	Some say accident. Some say the *harijans* are beaten… I walked fast. I met Prashant on the road. He told me to leave the place quickly.
Sudhir Babu	:	He said, and you came. So, I can't stay without thanking my educated son.
Leeli	:	Please understand. Don't control him at his in-law's house.
Kishore Babu	:	(smiling) The parents always behave similarly everywhere. Please don't take it seriously.

Badal	:	It doesn't matter to me. I know my dad well.
		[Sunayana calls him from inside.]
Sunayana	:	*Sumuduni,* please come inside.
Leeli	:	It doesn't seem to me that we will leave today. The road is blocked.
Kishore Babu	:	Yes, is there a power supply? Switch on the T.V.
		[The news in T. V. – Bomb explosion in Khandadiha. Some say the Maoists are involved in it. Some say a police investigation is going on…. The T.V. gets disconnected.]
Kishore Babu	:	Watching T. V. is over. Please bring the radio. Like old parents, the radio must be in the room for our touch. It may be out of order or without battery.
		[Sunayana enters.]
Sunayana	:	Do you know today's newspaper published that the girl Ranjita from the other lane has eloped with somebody?
Kishore Babu	:	If you read all this, how will you know about the national and international issues?
Sudhir Babu	:	Yes, that's true. Let me interfere here. One will be influenced by the incident that happens in the neighbourhood. Otherwise, he is not a normal person.
Sunayana	:	You are right, but to what extent can one be normal? (taking a long breath)
Leelidevi	:	Of what are you discussing, *Samuduni*?
Sudhir Babu	:	We should consider what *Samuduni* is saying. *Sumudi*! Do you know that our

	Chhanda's marriage has been cancelled? I am still calm and quiet. I returned today, checking my weak heart. Even after that, I am normal.
Leelidevi :	I visited my elder sister's house eight days earlier. I heard our Chhanda's marriage is cancelled. It's good that all our tensions vanished.
Sinu :	Dad and Mom, please come – I am serving food on the plate.
Kishore Babu :	Please sit here for a while, my daughter. What's the nickname of your younger sister?
Sunayana :	Have you forgotten her name within two days? She is Chhanda…
Sinu :	(Being ashamed of) No, Dad, that's nothing. (Badal enters.)
Kishore Babu :	Where have you gone? We are waiting for you here.
Badal :	Yes, what happened yesterday or the day before yesterday? Some conspiracies are plotted.
Sinu :	You are roaming somewhere and say conspiracy is plotted here.
Chhanda :	Yes, Uncle, regular conspiracy- I am saying. Could you pay attention to me?
Sinu :	Chhanda, let's move. We will serve on the dining table.
Kishore Babu :	You speak, Chhanda; you will be relieved. Don't listen to your sister-in-law.
Chhanda :	As I listened to her, I could save my life.
Suddhir Babu :	I can't understand what you are saying, my dear. (Sunayana enters.)

Sunayana	:	*Samudi*, our Chhanda, came here one or two days before.
Sudhir/Leeli	:	Why?
Sunayana	:	She needed her uncle's opinions.
Badal	:	What opinions?
Chhanda	:	Where the son at home obediently remains silent, not raising his voice against injustice or something wrong, I have some responsibility to execute.
Badal	:	Does it mean to be at the relative's house?
Kishore	:	Hello, my dear! She thought of us as her own. So, she came. Where could she go otherwise?
Sinu	:	I have sent her to my dad. She was not interested in marrying Manish. That's why I have sent him to my father.
Sudhir	:	Okay, *Samudi*, God has saved us.
Sunayana	:	When we were helpless and couldn't do anything, God took it seriously and punished that fellow heavily.
Badal	:	(To Sinu) That night, Was Chhanda telling you to call from my mobile?
Sinu	:	That day was my dad and mom's marriage anniversary. They told Chhanda to stay there. As she didn't inform us at home, she returned. She reminded me of my parents' marriage anniversary day, and you got the chance to become the most loved son-in-law. Do you understand now?
Sudhir	:	My daughter is intelligent. Please come to me. You are the golden bridge between two families. (Chhanda and Sinu look at each other.)

Sudhir	:	Both come – Try to prove that daughter and daughter-in-law at home are more than two sisters in friendship to those who say they are perpetual enemies.
Leelidevi	:	Yes, now I can understand. In my absence, my daughter-in-law manages our families well. She thinks about my daughter more than me and is very conscious of the family's pride and social prestige.
Kishore Babu	:	This is all possible for Sunayana's education-
Sunayana	:	(Being ashamed of) All parents teach their children well. But how many of them learn that? You all come- let me move to that side. (She leaves.)
Chhanda	:	But my *Bhauja* (daughter-in-law) is genuinely exceptional.
Badal	:	Don't praise your *Bhauja* (daughter-in-law) so much. She will swell in pride.
Sudhir	:	Yes, where you stayed aside, she strategically considered your responsibility and managed it nicely. ['Rice is served on the plate. Please come.' - Voice from inside]
Kishore Babu	:	*Sanudi*, the agitation on the road has put the innocent mob in trouble but has given us a chance for a family get-together. [Both moved, smiling happily.]

LAST SCENE

[All are in the drawing room after food.]

Kishore Babu : *Samudi*, please see I am not blaming you. The people of our generation are straightforward, innocent, gullible and easily believed in. But...

Sudhir Babu : Why did you stop? Please, carry on...

Kishore Babu : Have we been aware of our daughters' personalities? If we train them, they can improve their personality and step up the ladder of success. Can you imagine ever?

Leelidevi : What are you saying?

Kishore Babu : Please see, my daughter is your daughter-in-law. Interfering in your private affairs...

Leelidevi : Please say – you have already strengthened our relationship for one birth.

Kishore Babu : If Chhanda agrees to marry after two years of completing her Ph. D., won't it be good? She said that day, "She has already been registered for the course."

Sudhir Babu : It can be, but ...Now she is twenty-four. (Sunayana enters.)

Sunayana : Who is twenty-four now? Is it to our Chhanda? Okay, she can get married at twenty-six or twenty-seven. (Sinu calls from inside.) You can come here; your dad and father-in-law are gossiping here. (Sinu comes.)

Sinu : Dad, are you worried? Who knew that the road would be blocked?

Sudhir Babu : Hey, daughter! Your dad says, "Let

		Chhanda marry after completing her Ph. D. What's your opinion?
Sinu	:	I have already told your son that repeatedly, Dad.
Sudhir Babu	:	Oh, he has never told me that.
Sinu	:	He needs to be convinced first, before convincing you.
Leelidevi	:	Let me ask first my daughter whether she loves anybody.
Sinu	:	Mom, you don't take it otherwise. You have started discussing. You are Chhanda's mother. Have you ever given Chhanda any time to spell out her opinion? Have you ever discussed anything with her in detail?
Leelidevi	:	Please stop – don't say anything more. I confess you are my worthy daughter-in-law. You have saved my family's pride and prestige. What more can I say?
Sudhir Babu	:	Leave all that – (Please come here, Chhanda)
Chhanda	:	Dad, did you call me?
Sudhir Babu	:	My dear, express yourself before us without inhibitions. Do you love anybody?
Chhanda	:	Dad, what are you saying?
Sinu	:	Dad, if Chhanda loved somebody, how would you accept her/that? You speak honestly.
Kishore Babu	:	Hey, if their daughter loved an employed son of their caste, her parents would appreciate her for two reasons. First, she saved the prestige of their family;

secondly, they accomplished their daughter's marriage without dowry/with less dowry.
[He laughs with his romantic expression.]

Chhanda : I have obeyed my dad's decision to date. My *Bhauja* (daughter-in-law) has influenced me for the last five to seven years. I have learnt much from her about how one must sacrifice oneself to build a family. Am I in my teens now? (Badal enters.)

Badal : Well, I have a question for my younger sister (To Chhanda): Can you get married to whom I should choose?

Chhanda : No, I won't accept anybody unquestioningly.

Badal : Are you sure? Think of it twice.

Sinu : Why are you teasing her? Can I know?

Badal : Oh, why are you interfering between us? Well, if that boy were Chandan from the class just above yours,

Chhanda : Chandan?

Badal : Why are you silent now? Your sister-in-law, advocating for you, needs to learn about the matter.

Chhanda : *Bhai* (brother) –

Badal : Hey, After I heard from you, I moved towards the market. I met Chandan there. As I told him that you had come, he was happy. I came here with his scooter.

Sinu : You are great. After a long time, you have understood your responsibility as the son and brother.

Leelidevi	:	I need to find out who is great here. Where is Chandan? (Badal accompanies Chandan from outside.)
Chandan	:	Namaskar, sir – I am very fortunate to meet you all.
Leelidevi	:	My dear boy! What do you say? Your parents?
Sudhir Babu	:	Go and prepare some snacks for him.
Sinu	:	Yes, I am going, Dad – Mom, please be here.
Badal	:	Mom, you see whether you like him or not.
Kishore Babu	:	But I have understood everything. My dear, I know you are on the verge of completing your thesis. Your family depends on you, and so is your sister's responsibility. Nobody forces you to accept Chhanda right now. Take your own time. Then…
Chandan	:	I don't understand how all these things are happening.
Sudhir Babu	:	Well, think of it for a while. At least you relieve me from the blemishes. Closing my eyes, I am the father sending his daughter to another's house.
Leelidevi	:	How will you make this significant decision before I return home from the relative's house?
Badal	:	Leave all that. Let them have an interaction for a while. Let's go inside. (They left Chhanda there.)
Chhanda	:	Chandan Babu!
Chandan	:	You have addressed me as 'Babu' for

		many days. Now you say whether you can live with me for your entire life.
Chhanda	:	Silence–
Chandan	:	Can I understand your silence as 'yes'?
Chanda	:	Do you know how difficult it is to build a family? When my parents and my brother agreed on this, …
Chandan	:	And you? I never thought my life's decision would be made this way. I have no objection to accepting you as my life partner. (Sinu comes with a plate filled with snacks.)
Sinu	:	But I have an objection.
Chanda	:	*Bhauja* (Sister-in-law) …
Sinu	:	You are gossiping with Chandan Babu, and we … we all…
Chhanda	:	You have saved my life, *Bhauja*.
Sinu	:	Okay, I will tell my dad that your son has done an excellent job, which will be remembered for a long time. [Badal enters.]
Badal	:	Let me know what lecture you are delivering here. Let's go inside. We must be ready to leave the place once the agitation is called off on the road.
Sinu	:	No need to be hurried. You are the elder brother. Who will look after the younger brother-in-law's responsibility?
Chandan	:	You should not think of me here. Please excuse me; I want to say a line. When a son and a daughter-in-law like you are in the family, there won't be any question of generation gap.

		[Sudhir Babu enters.]
Sudhir Babu	:	You are right; you could understand everything well in advance. Now, it's time to focus on the children's choices. We must believe in them.
Chhanda	:	Yes, Dad, one should not discriminate between a son and a daughter. [Leelidevi enters.]
Leelidevi	:	Yes, you shouldn't think of a daughter as a burden, so hurry to free yourself from it by arranging her marriage with anyone without enquiring about that stranger and consulting your wife.
Sinu	:	One important point is to be noted at this moment. A daughter is never a burden, and a daughter like Chhanda can't be a burden.

END

Our Geeti: Our Pride

Dramatis Personae

Prasant Babu	:	Retired Govt. Servant, Age: 65-68
Tushar	:	Prasant Babu's son, Engineer, Age: 28
Shanti Devi	:	Wife of Prasant Babu, Age: 60-62
Giti	:	Tushar's wife, Age: 24
Swati	:	Geeti's younger sister, Age: 22

SCENE- I

[It is Giti's *Asthamagala*. (Eighth day after her marriage). There would have been many people in the house, but because of Covid-19, everything had gone quiet. No grand celebration: she came like that only. It is evening, and the news is on the television. Shanti Devi, Giti's mother-in-law, gives a call.]

Shanti Devi : Hey, did you hear? There is an announcement of a storm. It might cause havoc. (Prasant Babu replies.)

Prasant Babu : I will always go berserk hearing this COVID news. Now, the storm has come – I won't be able to go.

Shanti Devi	:	As if the storm would stop if you didn't watch. [calling Giti] Dear Giti! Would you bring a cup of tea?
Giti	:	Okay, Mom. [coming with two cups of tea] I have added ginger to it, Mom – especially now.
Shanti Devi	:	Good! I can understand what your parents must be feeling. [Caressing the daughter-in-law]
Giti	:	What can we do, Mom? We must cope with everything that happens. [Prasant Babu arrives.]
Prasant Babu	:	Oh, Dear, I returned to have the tea. Whatever your mother-in-law says, don't take it to heart. She had a wish to welcome her daughter-in-law with a huge celebration. She wanted everyone in the village to attend the grand reception. It was her dream, so she is disheartened.
Giti	:	Leave it, dad! I only need your blessings so I can fit into this new family well.
Shanti Devi	:	Yes, dear! Your father-in-law said everything about my dream -I am only the bad person here. Your parents must be disappointed too, aren't they?
Giti	:	Yes, Mom! My mother told me yesterday that all the preparations were unsuccessful for this COVID-19 only.
Shanti Devi	:	Where has our Tushar gone? I can't see him. (Tushar enters.)
Tushar	:	Mom, there is nowhere to go except sticking our faces to the computers.
Prasant Babu	:	Hey Tushar! Our daughter-in-law works

		somewhere, doesn't she? What kind of work is it?
Tushar	:	She has a Ph.D. in Social Science from Delhi University. There, she worked part-time. Since the lockdown, everything has gone to rest.
Shanti Devi	:	Good! At least you two will get time to be together. I have gained weight.
Prasant Babu	:	Shanti, start doing a little exercise. At least try doing *Anulom Vilom*. (A Yoga breathing exercise or the alternate nostril breathing)
Shanti Devi	:	Earlier, I used to go to the parks; now, even that much isn't allowed. We can't even walk on the streets for any significant reason. What should we do now?
Giti	:	Mom, I will say one more thing. You and Dad should start playing ludo. Do word-making or listen to devotional songs from YouTube.
Shanti Devi	:	No, my dear, he never considers me a friend; why don't you ask him?
Giti	:	(laughing) (to Tushar) Do bring a ludo when you go to the market to buy vegetables. You will play if it is kept aside.
Prasant Babu	:	Oh, God! Your mother is a sore loser. She cries or gets grumpy if she loses – (laughing)
Tushar	:	No, Giti, my mom is not a sore loser. Come on, let's play Ludo starting tomorrow.
Shanti Devi	:	I don't even have time to read Bhagavat. Who would play ludo? Leave this topic

	– let's go, kids; I need to bless you and complete all the *Asthamangala* rituals. (Everyone leaves.)
Prasant Babu :	(Chuckling) Isn't it funny? Everyone's saying the same thing these days: if things don't go your way, it's bound to lead to arguments—thank you, Corona! Now here we are, all stuck at home, doing absolutely nothing for no good reason!

SCENE- II

(Two days later. Giti is extremely joyous after getting the mail.)

Tushar	:	You seem pleased – what happened?
Giti	:	I got a scholarship from Harvard University. Look!
Tushar	:	You have never told me this.
Giti	:	Last year, nobody could go from India because of COVID-19. This time, I must manage somehow.
Tushar	:	What about mom?
Giti	:	Leave it to me; it's my responsibility to convince her.
		(Shanti Devi was passing by - stops.)
Shanti Devi	:	How will you convince your mom? Let me listen to you first.
Giti	:	Mom, I will go abroad to study higher studies. I just received the mail.
Shanti Devi	:	You have already studied so much; what else is left to study? Is that programme not here in India? In foreign countries? Let me go. (She leaves.)
Giti	:	Yes, Mom. It's my dream to study at

		Harvard. Please don't say no.
Tushar	:	Are you sure you will go?
Giti	:	Yes. How can't you understand?
Tushar	:	Let me ask Dad. (calls dad) dad…. Dad…. (Dad comes holding the newspaper.)
Prasant Babu	:	What's the matter, son? Why are you calling me like this?
Tushar	:	Our Giti will go to Harvard University to get her doctorate.
Prasant Babu	:	Wow! It is such good news. Congratulations, my dear. You are the pride of our family.
Giti	:	(Touching his feet) With your blessings, I will keep our name high there, Dad.
Prasant Babu	:	(Calling Shanti Devi) Shanti, did you hear? Our Giti will go abroad. Such a huge offer is just right after the marriage – it's our fortune -where is she? (Shanti Devi comes. Giti and Tushar go outside together.)
Shanti Devi	:	I don't like to recall those unpleasant talks. You keep on praising your daughter-in-law.
Prasant Babu	:	It will take six months to prepare all the paperwork. Do you think she will leave tomorrow or on the 16th day of her marriage?
Shanti Devi	:	Everything is shut for Corona. Why is their international organization not closed?
Prasant Babu	:	We will see….
Shanti Devi	:	You forbade them from bringing any dowry. Even the good sweets she

		couldn't bring. Thanks to Corona, and they even get the clothes for gifting the family members!
Prasant Babu	:	That's enough. You also owe her a wedding feast, remember? You didn't even make any ornaments for your daughter-in-law. This isn't just our problem; it's something the world faces. You should be grateful to God for getting a daughter like Giti.
Giti	:	Mom, my mother is on video call. Talk to her, please.
Shanti Devi	:	I don't know how to use that stupid thing. Can't you tell her that?
Giti	:	(Passing the phone to Shanti Devi) (Giti's mom's voice) Hello, *Samudini* (To Shanti's mother-in-law) how have you been? Geeti is no longer just my daughter—she's yours now. Please treat her as your own. Now that she's off to go abroad, you can decide as you feel. We're doing well here, so don't worry. Please give my regards to Prasant Babu. (The call hangs up.)
Shanti Devi	:	That's it! Enough of all this sweet talk. I've already spoken to your dad and mom about everything.
Giti	:	(Crying) Whatever you say, I'll do, Mom. Please don't be upset. I can't bear to see you angry.
Shanti Devi	:	So, you wasted no time telling your mom about going abroad, did you? Honestly, these kids can't keep anything to themselves.

Giti	:	My letter came to our house first, Mom. Swati forwarded it here. They found out the news before I could say anything—I didn't tell them anything.
Prasant Babu	:	Don't her parents have their share of happiness in their daughter's achievement? They've played a part in her success, too. Don't be disheartened, Shanti. The way we behave impacts on our children, you know. I've told you before that times have changed. (He moves away.)

SCENE- III

(A Week later, Evening. Tushar has returned from the office; Geeti takes the bag from his hand.)

Tushar	:	Geeti, please sit, we need to talk
Geeti	:	Wait a second. I have put the tea on the boil. Let me serve it to Mom and Dad; I will get a cup for you, and then we will chat. (She leaves.)
Tushar	:	(To himself) How should a newlywed behave? Why is she so detached? At least I can be a little happy. (Phone rings) Hello!! Yes, I have just arrived. I will have a conversation with Giti, and I have a lot of work after that – (Giti comes with the tea.)
Tushar	:	You won't be able to recognize her; she is a friend of mine. Although I am in Odisha Administrative Service, she is a management expert. She walks around

		taking classes and doesn't even ask for the money she gets ……….
Giti	:	Leave it; why must we talk about her money? Say what you want to say.
Tushar	:	I don't know how to say obliquely. So get straight to the point. Is it important to go to Harvard?
Giti	:	What?! I thought you would be happy, so, aren't you?
Giti	:	A friend of mine was talking about her brother and sister-in-law. Her sister-in-law is a nice girl. She knew the art of making strangers her own. She went abroad without her family's approval.
Giti	:	Oh, …That friend is filling your head with all that poison.
Tushar	:	Hear - she was so focused on her career that she aborted her child when she was pregnant and didn't even tell anyone.
Giti	:	Then?
Tushar	:	Now, she is serving in the States (the USA) and doesn't even want to return.
Giti	:	Yes, she must have fallen in love with a blonde gentleman.
Tushar	:	How did you know?
Giti	:	It is simple – her husband must have gone mad, and his family might have already started looking for a new girl. (laughing)
Tushar	:	You find it funny, right? Here, my soul has been choked.
Giti	:	First, I am never going to abort my baby if I am planning for a baby in a year or so. Secondly, I am very homesick.

Tushar	:	If you are homesick, don't leave the house, my baby; please listen to me.
Giti	:	See, my childhood dream was to study abroad. You are my lucky charm; otherwise, how did I get this scholarship right after our marriage?
Tushar	:	But …I….
Giti	:	It is just a matter of two years. It will pass in the blink of an eye. Mom, Dad, and you are coming. We will move around in Delhi for a week. Then, seeing me off, you will come back.
Tushar	:	I don't know why, but I am not convinced.
Giti	:	You have studied so much – I understand Mom's concern.
		(Then comes Shanti Devi.)
Shanti Devi	:	Why have I become the topic of discussion here?
Tushar	:	No, Mom, it's nothing like that.
Giti	:	What 'no'? Mom, please sit here. I want to ask both of you a question.
Shanti Devi	:	Okay, Mom! (speaking gaily) – this is your family -see, don't ask me anything complicated – I don't remember anything and not well-read like you.
Giti	:	Wouldn't you have been happy if your son had gotten the letter about going abroad?
Shanti Devi	:	Why is this question? If we had heard of our son going abroad, we would have arranged a feast, worshipped the village Goddess, etc.
Giti	:	So, why are you sad about your daughter-in-law going abroad?

Tushar	:	You don't know, Giti, how much pain my mom holds. My sister was about to attend the Central University of Hyderabad, but her in-laws didn't allow that.
Shanti Devi	:	(With sobbing and wiping eyes) Don't scratch old wounds. Giti won't understand, but this will upset me even more.
Giti	:	I will understand, Mom. You are also a mother. I know how much painful it might be for you to witness your daughter's premature death. But what's my fault with that? Can't you convince yourself by sending me abroad to study higher? I will become another Itu *Apa*. (She cries.)
Shanti Devi	:	My daughter! Why are you crying? Go to wash your face – you both should go and visit your house. You might feel good.
Giti	:	How will we go in this lockdown, Mom? I will prepare to leave if you won't feel upset – otherwise …….
Shanti Devi	:	Otherwise, what? You will go. Two years will end in just a blink of an eye – also, I am not dying so soon.
Tushar	:	Why do you always talk like this? Why won't we go around and with that, we can visit her university as well?
Shanti Devi	:	No, your dad won't be able to stay alone. If you want to go, you can. You can stay there for eight days, then return. Let her friends know how her husband is— bestowed by all the great qualities she has been.

Giti	:	Come with us, Mom. Every child is beautiful in the eyes of their mother.
Tushar	:	Now Okay. Let's send the mail. We need to know all the details
Shanti Devi	:	Yes, go. Oh, Maa Mangala! Take care of my children (She prays, closing her hands.)

SCENE- IV

(Swati gets out of the auto around 4.00 pm. She rings the bell.)

Giti	:	(Opening the door) Is it you, Swati? Wait there! Please don't jump on me; the time isn't good.
Swati	:	Good! Following all COVID protocols. "If you obey and respect others' words, your condition will improve."

(While smiling, she greets Shanti Devi and Prasant Babu.)

Swati	:	Aunty, I have come to see you.
Prasant Babu	:	Oh, dear! How did you come? Did they allow you to go from home?
Swati	:	I came to a friend's house. While returning, I remembered my Giti *Apa* a lot. Then, I came.
Prasant Babu	:	You are studying in Vani Vihar, right? Which subject?
Swati	:	It's Political Science. Everything has been closed for a year. We are just studying online. I went to get a few books from my friend's house. Apa, Apa, Giti Apa, where are you? Whenever I say you are busy,

		you hang the call – you have become such a housewife.
Giti	:	(Coming) I was getting snacks for you. You like *pakoras*, don't you?
Swati	:	Sit here – (Making her sit) You are going to Harvard. I have gone crazy with joy after hearing this news. Apa, you're fortunate. Harvard's library is the world's best; you can see the road through the net.
Prasant Babu	:	Dear, we are lucky too – our daughter-in-law got such great news as soon as she came. I would have distributed sweets if it wasn't COVID time. (Shanti Devi burst into laughter.)
Shanti Devi	:	Whom would you have given the sweets? We couldn't even get sweets from our daughter-in-law's house.
Prasant Babu	:	Don't say such things. You have a talking doll, yet you ask for more sweets. There is a variety of sweets available on the market. Anybody may say anything; I could never understand you. How could you name Shanti?
Shanti Devi	:	It's just a slip of the tongue. You are teasing me a lot.
Swati	:	Aunty, sometimes what is in mind comes out of the mouth.
Shanti Devi	:	Don't think much, dear. We are all sitting in the same fire.
Swati	:	Mom was worried, too. Once Corona goes, she will call the bride and groom and will depart them with all respect.

		(Tushar comes, and Swati touches her feet as a sign of respect.)
Tushar	:	What respect? To whom?
Swati	:	You won't understand, *Jiju*. My sister studies "Third World Economic Development", don't you know? She will make you understand – (laughing at her romanticism)
Shanti Devi	:	Your in-laws will invite you to their home to show respect.
Tushar	:	But their daughter is ready to leave abroad- and............
Swati	:	Your wife should be your pride, *Jiju*. You are lucky to have such a wife.
Prasant Babu	:	I will tell you one thing: my son is very outdated.
Swati	:	No, uncle, my brother-in-law is great. He stands out from the rest. My father takes a lot of pride while talking about his son-in-law.
Tushar	:	Leave it. You should have packed your sister's bag, and now I will do it. We must scale everything we put in the bag; otherwise, we will be fined at the airport. She would have returned fifteen days or a month from your house, but now it will take two years.
Swati	:	Oh! Is that difficult? There is a professor who lives alone on the campus. His wife and children live away from him. We jokingly call him "Married Bachelor" – good!
Shanti Devi	:	Leave this topic – dear (Swati), you will stay here today, right?

Swati	:	No, Aunty, my uncle will return around 7–7:30 pm. So, I will go with him; it is just an hour's distance anyway. I came, but would he like to come down here? (Giti calls her from inside.)
Prasant Babu	:	Hey dear! Let's go, your sister is calling inside.
Shanti Devi	:	(Looking at the clock) It will be 6 O'clock soon. Come dear – what would the new bride be doing alone? (Going inside)
Swati	:	Aunty, say anything, but you are very caring and affectionate. My sister Giti is very fortunate.
Prasant Babu	:	Yes, dear, Giti is also a decent girl. Yes, family values – not everyone gets it.
Tushar	:	Swati, did you see how concerned my parents are for you and your sister? Moreover, I was only there to drop my luggage off at the airport.
Swati	:	After all, she is Mrs. Tushar Samantray. Where do we get in between? Now too much crowd isn't allowed in the airports. (Going inside laughing)
Tushar	:	I smell pakoras. I am going too. (Stop) you said right, Swati- let's see where my life takes me. (Prasant Babu comes.)
Prasant Babu	:	What are you saying alone, Tushar?
Tushar	:	No, dad
Prasant Babu	:	Hey! If you had this chance to go abroad, Giti would have lit a lamp continuously for you – you would have been trapped somewhere …….
Tushar	:	Dad!

Prasant Babu	:	Those blondes in America like Indian boys.
Tushar	:	Stop it, Dad. Otherwise, Giti, Swati and Mom will come to give advice.
Prasant Babu	:	You are so kind and considerate. Take this event as a matter of pride. Not everyone gets such glory. Let's go – Swati will leave.

SCENE- V

(Tushar leaves for the office at 10.00 am, and Shanti Sevi comes.)

Shanti Devi	:	Oh, Dear! I have received ten calls since this morning, flooded with good wishes.
Tushar	:	Who all have called you, Mom?
Shanti Devi	:	All my friends from the park. My sister, Mrs. Dash. Your father's friend's wife and our ladies' club president.
Tushar	:	My phone is filled with congratulation messages. Such news spreads fast.
Shanti Devi	:	So? Nobody has stolen anything. Let people know how studious my daughter-in-law is. (Prasant Babu enters.)
Prasant Babu	:	Did you see! He who steals and tries to hide it eventually gets caught. (laughing)
Shanti Devi	:	Why are you so ruthless all the time – has nobody congratulated you?
Prasant Babu	:	Of course! People have congratulated me – we are retired people. Measuring our happiness is difficult. Anyway, after getting so many messages, you have released that Giti is the pride of our family. Have faith in her – motivate her.

Tushar	:	Right, Dad, trusting the whispers of a stranger might be poisonous to our soul. After all, Giti is my wife.
Prasant Babu	:	Wah! – right son, a woman is the one who saves from the destruction – you understand.
Tushar	:	I am leaving for the office. (Phone rings.) Hello Swati! We have been waiting for your call since the morning. I hope you are safe. Give my best wishes to Mom and Dad. Do visit us when you come next. I will ask your sister to call you. (He went outside and got on his motorcycle.)
Giti	:	Mom, you take two to three days to think – why so worried? I will deny it. Without your blessings, can I go, or can I concentrate on my studies there? I am leaving. (He moved.)
Prasant Babu	:	Hey, poor children have become depressed after listening to your words.
Shanti Devi	:	It's better if she cries instead of leaving the house.
Prasant Babu	:	You have seen the world enough, Shanti. Let her go. They will build their world. Why are you spoiling your name? Instead, convince Tushar.
Shanti Devi	:	He is roaming around with a sad face.
Prasant Babu	:	How I will thank you, mother-son duo! -Everyone will learn how to talk madly from him. (Sound of stopping of the motorcycle) Maybe Tushar has come. Open the door. (Shanti Devi opens the door.)

Tushar	:	What are you thinking, Mom? Whoever is listening to this news has one thing to say: that Giti should leave for abroad with a happy mind; people are asking me for a treat.
Shanti Devi	:	Okay, then she may go; if you are convinced, who are we to say anything?
Prasant Babu	:	Well! This pair of mother and son! Learn to be happy with daughter-in-law's achievement. (They went away.)
Shanti Devi	:	Hey Corona! Hey Storm! At least some should consider my case – I can't deal with this anymore.
Tushar	:	Don't break me now. All of us should support Giti; let's stop this matter here.
Shanti Devi	:	Explain to me what she is going to study.
Tushar	:	She is going to pursue higher studies in economic development. You will only understand when she will be treated with high regard after her return.
Shanti Devi	:	Can I wait forever without any work for her to return?
Tushar	:	Don't dishearten yourself like that, Mom. Try to be a little happy.

LAST SCENE

(Prasant Babu and Shanti Devi are sitting in the front yard. Prasant Babu is reading the newspaper)

Prasant Babu	:	This CORONA-19 took away many of our people quickly.
Shanti Devi	:	Yes, these married folks are leaving; it hurts. I wish I had gone.
Prasant Babu	:	Have you gone mad, Shanti?

Shanti Devi	:	Could we not refuse our daughter-in-law? If I leave for the heavenly abode during Corona, she will automatically cancel going abroad. It would be very nice.
Prasant Babu	:	Oh, dear God! Nobody can make you understand – trying to convince you to do something is worthless.
Shanti Devi	:	Isn't she scared? She will go alone and stay for two years. Who knows how that place is?
Prasant Babu	:	Our Giti is a mature girl. She won't do anything wrong. otherwise ….
Shanti Devi	:	Otherwise, what?
Prasant Babu	:	Otherwise, who prepares to go abroad just after getting married, you say?
Shanti Devi	:	Right. I was struck by Giti's question that day. Son's going abroad is a matter of joy, whereas it's hard for a daughter-in-law to leave for abroad. Indeed, I didn't think of this. (Giti comes.)
Giti	:	Won't you take a little rest today, Dad? – Let me bring ludo.
Prasant Babu	:	Dear, sit here. After you leave abroad, what will we do except play ludo? (laughing)
Giti	:	I am telling you to write about your childhood days. All the highs and lows you have endured and passed through together will be comforting.
Shanti Devi	:	Should I visit my village at the end of the month?
Shanti Devi	:	I will return without a whisper. You expect me to howl about it, don't you?

Prasant Babu	:	You will have to stay in quarantine after returning for at least two weeks, and then you will come home.
Shanti Devi	:	Oh, my God! Then, I cancelled my visit to my father's house.
Giti	:	Dad, he (Tushar) was saying to visit the Jagannath Temple once it opens.
Shanti Devi	:	This touched my heart. My son is very intelligent.
Prasant Babu	:	Intelligent or a pushover? He is unduly upset about someone else's sister-in-law not returning from abroad.
Giti	:	So, have you heard everything?
Prasant Babu	:	Yes dear! I have heard about her – all about you.
Giti	:	Still, I have tried to make him understand, Dad- this opportunity won't come again. If there's mutual understanding, then nothing can affect us. We shall undoubtedly set an example for others.
Shanti Devi	:	This duo, father and daughter-in-law, talk the same.
Prasant Babu	:	Shanti, teach our daughter-in-law how to cook.
Shanti Devi	:	Why? Will she snatch the spatula from my hand to cook the food?
Prasant Babu	:	She will stay alone! And no one knows better than you how to make a dish more delicious.
Giti	:	Mom, you say – I will note it down – then I will make it as convenient.
Shanti Devi	:	Dear, can I ask you a question? You won't get angry, right?

Giti	:	Please ask, Mom.
Shanti Devi	:	Do you have to go? You have made our home filled with happiness. At least we hear your anklets' sound. Otherwise, you two humans used to live in dead sound.
Giti	:	Your son is here.
Prasant Babu	:	Our Tushar? He is all for his friends and the market. He is always on his mobile.

(Giti comes. She hums. Shanti Devi comes as well.)

Shanti Devi	:	Oh dear! Finish your work. You also must prepare. You have an online interview, don't you?
Giti	:	You remember, mom?
Shanti Devi	:	Yes, dear, if only Iti Apa had gone away to study, she would have been with us. I promise I will make sure you pursue your doctorate. In this way, I can find some redemption for all this.

(Prasant Babu comes.)

Prasant Babu	:	Shanti, what redemption are you doing? Stay a little calm during this time of Corona. Pray to God. Our children should live for each other. Even if we live in difficulty, there must not be any misunderstanding between the children.
Giti	:	I can do anything with your blessings, Dad- please convince your son.
Prasant Babu	:	He understood. You don't need to stay in any dilemma. This house is yours; you must take on all the responsibilities once you return because we have grown old and don't have much time.
Shanti Devi	:	Hey, will you cook food here after

		studying so much? Will you rear the cows or ranch cattle? Will you boil paddy or pound the grains?
Prasant Babu	:	You are struck there, Shanti. Wherever our daughter-in-law stays, that will be her home. *'Vasudhaiva Kutumbakam.'* [The whole world is a family.]
Shanti Devi	:	Spare me with this. At least if she had kids, it would have made some sense. (Tushar comes.)
Tushar	:	Let's leave this topic right here. Now, we must prepare ourselves. I know my parents are very modern.
Shanti Devi	:	It's nice -if everyone is giving so much gravity to this matter, why shouldn't we? Honestly speaking, our Giti is our wealth/pride. Hey, Giti. Give your mother a video call. Hello! *Samuduni* (To Giti's mother), you should repeat after me, our Giti is our pride.

END

Suchana: The Name of a Girl

Dramatis Personae

Narasingha Babu	:	Retired Police Officer
Nayan/Nanu	:	Narasingha Babu's son
Surya	:	Son-in-law of Narasingha Babu and Suchi's husband
Nirmala Devi	:	Wife of Narasingha Babu
Suchana	:	The youngest daughter
Archana	:	Another daughter

SCENE-I

(It's evening. While Narasingha Babu, a retired police officer, watches the news on TV, his wife, Nirmala Devi, enters.)

Nirmala : Did you watch the news? Could you turn the TV off for a while? I want to talk to you.

Narasingha : It's hard to believe, but it's been forty years since we married. Over the years,

		I've heard so much, and many of those voices have faded away. What's on your mind today?
Nirmala	:	You're right. I've never really had the freedom to speak my mind. I've spent my day listening to our children's words and those of our parents, siblings, and relatives.
Narasingha	:	Alright, what's bothering you?
Nirmala	:	I haven't heard from Suchi in a while, which makes me uneasy.
Narasingha	:	Oh, Mr. Adhikari, our son-in-law, is a responsible family man. He excels in everything, be it politics or business. We're fortunate.
Nirmala	:	That's true, but couldn't Suchi at least call us once?
Narasingha	:	She's probably busy. Don't worry, we'll call her tomorrow morning.
Nirmala	:	It feels like just yesterday when Bandana was six, Archana was three and a half, and I was expecting again. Everyone predicted it would be a boy for sure.
Narasingha	:	(chuckling) Yes, that's why I named our daughter Suchana, meaning "information."
Nirmala	:	Everyone was teasing that day. Remember?
Narasingha	:	And then we were blessed with a son, Nayan. His friends used to tease him by calling him Nayana. I remember it all.
Nirmala	:	Where is Nayan? He's so far away that my eyes can't reach him. He should at

		least answer the phone. Has he finished his studies yet?
Narasingha	:	Bandana's son must have started his higher education. She's not free to come over instantly.
Nirmala	:	But...
Narasingha	:	And Archana, she's in Bangalore with her husband, who holds a high position. She's invited us to visit many times.
Nirmala	:	Forget it. Didn't Archana say she'd visit us during the holidays? Ask her when she's coming and how long she'll stay.
Narasingha	:	She's lived in this house for almost twenty-three to twenty-four years. We can't expect her to stay for long now. I'll ask her when she's coming tomorrow morning if you insist.
Nirmala	:	Oh God! What made you so laid-back?
Narasingha	:	After a lifetime of carrying burdens, let me take things lightly now. How many struggles, misunderstandings, and ups and downs have we faced?
Nirmala	:	Okay, that's enough.
Narasingha	:	How far are we with the food preparations? What was that boy's name again? He'll return home once his work is done...
Nirmala	:	You can turn the TV back on. I'll check. I'll bring the food here, and we can eat while watching a serial.
Narasingha	:	Good. (Nirmala leaves. The phone rings) Hello... hello... who is this? Archi... Your mother was talking about you. When? Archi, I can't hear you properly. Have

	you booked the tickets? Then? Your mother will be thrilled to listen to this. Nirmala, can you hear? Come here; Archi is on the line.
Nirmala	: (coming back) Let me hold... (picking up the phone) Hello... Archi... Archi... Maybe the call got disconnected. It's just my luck... I won't see any happiness in this lifespan.
Narasingha	: She'll be here by the fifteenth of this month. It's the third day today. She called to confirm her ticket. You have about twelve days to prepare.
Nirmala	: That's fine, but could you also check on Suchi? Nanu has been here for two days, just sleeping all day and night. He changes the topic whenever I ask him to visit his sister. And Archana last saw Suchi in December 2007 when she got married. It's been three years.
Narasingha	: Why are you worrying so much? It's normal for siblings to meet less frequently after marriage. Okay, I'll investigate it.
Nirmala	: Why did you send our son Nanu so far away for his studies? What's his fault in all this? What can he do?
Narasingha	: Why don't you say I have sent him instead of driving him away from here? Think of it as preparing him for the competitive world out there. Nirmala, try to understand the challenges in today's world. To thrive, you must work hard all your life. How will you

		live if you are tired and disappointed so early?
Nirmala	:	Let's give the TV a break until nine-thirty. I'll check on that boy. I was also thinking...
Narasingha	:	What's up now?
Nirmala	:	I wanted to dust off the Bhagavat books and read a few verses daily.
Narasingha	:	That's a beautiful idea. My grandmother used to make me do the same. My father corrected me whenever I mispronounced the verses. Let's start afresh.

SCENE-II

(Narasingha Babu calls someone. The time is five O'clock in the evening.)

Narasingha	:	Hello! Dear, are you not at home? Your absence made us worried. When are you arriving? Will you stay here for a few days? Hold on, let me inform your mother. (Nanu, also known as Nayan enters.)
Nanu	:	Dad, who called?
Narasingha	:	Your sister Suchi. She and her husband have been away for fifteen days. They're returning now.
Nanu	:	When? Where did they go? (Nirmala enters.)
Nirmala	:	Why didn't you call me? When is she coming back?
Narasingha	:	They return after visiting several hill stations like Shimla and Dalhousie.

Nirmala	:	They'll stay here for four to five days. That's a relief. It's good that the kids went somewhere.
Nanu	:	(Calculating) Suchi will be back on the thirteenth, Archi will arrive on the fifteenth, and I'll return on the seventeenth. It'll be nice to have a couple of days together.
Nirmala	:	Excellent. I'll clean the house, especially since he's the new son-in-law.
Nanu	:	The elder son-in-law will also be here. For more information, visit our website, www.xyz.com.
Narasingha	:	Not all information is available on that website, my boy.
Nanu	:	Dad, do you remember when you asked me for the English word "information" when I was a child? I couldn't answer, and Suchi immediately looked it up in the dictionary and said, "Information". I even felt scolded at her behest.
Narasingha	:	I remember everything, dear.
Nanu	:	I teased her by calling her "Information Apa" for a long time.
Nirmala	:	(Laughing) This is our happiness. Every parent wishes for their children to get along well.
Nanu	:	Mom, there are even funnier stories. When her marriage was arranged, I teased her a lot. After seeing the Adhikari title, I called her Suchana Adhikari (Information Officer).

Narasingha	:	Yes, how long was the Right to Information Act? It started in 2005. I never thought of that.
Nanu	:	Dad, there are many stories like this. Let her arrive first, and then I'll ask her about her Right to Information.
Nirmala	:	Son! You will only ask her a few questions. Her husband will be with her. After all, he is our son-in-law.
Nanu	:	Mom, do you doubt my judgment?
Narasingha	:	First, go and help your mom with her household work. Call someone to clean the house.
Nirmala	:	Alright, dear, I'm leaving now. You were saying something about why worry, right? They've been in this house for so long. Why are you worried so much now?
Narasingha	:	I was saying, but...
Nirmala	:	God is great... truly great.
Narasingha	:	Don't tell me again what elements God has made you. Those phrases and cliches have been stored in my memory, hearing you repeatedly.
Nirmala	:	Alright, go to withdraw some money from the bank. It's good to have cash on hand.
Narasingha	:	Oh, I forgot to mention. One of our L.I.C. policies will mature this month.
Nirmala	:	You forgot to mention such important information but would instead ask me a hundred times what to wear and eat. If anyone heard, they'd be amazed! What

	a husband he is! He asks his wife for everything.
Narasingha :	Alright, dear, I forgot. I apologize. I can't apologize enough and can't do sit-ups because my knees are weak.
Nirmala :	Have you ever done sit-ups? If you had, would you say that? Women will always be women, no matter their age.
Nanu :	(from inside) Mom, please hold the table for me. It's wobbly. Please get me a towel; I'll tie it around my head.
Nirmala :	I have to help this father and son duo with everything. Alright, I'm coming.
Narasingha :	Oh, my God! It's like the temple bells ringing before entering. Yes, your daughter and son-in-law are coming.
Nirmala :	As if they are related only to me and not to you. Why do you get into hot water? Come on, Nanu, let's not stand here and get into silly fights. Arguments and counterarguments will be continued. (They left.)
Narasingha :	You don't understand, Nirmala. You have yet to see real fights. We went to many places together just a few months after getting married, and now I'm retired, we're finally resting in this city house. How would you understand the pain of those fights? I've seen heads being smashed and endured the troubles of the court. (He sighs deeply.) Those days were terrifying.

SCENE-III

(The house is crowded. Suchana and her husband have come.)

Nanu	:	Suchi Didi, did you fly with your hubby?
Suchi	:	Yes.
Nanu	:	Ah, that must have been exciting. I wish I had married Mr. Surya. You're lucky.
Surya	:	Flying isn't considered a status symbol anymore. You'll fly once you finish your studies. Why worry about it now?
Nanu	:	True, our family is more concerned about the cost of AC, non-AC, two-tier, three-tier; who has time to think about flight tickets?
Surya	:	Nanu, did you like your gift? You two can talk while I take a stroll in the market. (He leaves.)
Nanu	:	Sister, how much did the flight ticket cost?
Suchi	:	I don't know. Why didn't you ask him?
Nanu	:	Well, Shimla must be crowded with tourists now. Where did you guys stay?
Suchi	:	We stayed at a five-star hotel. It was very posh, oh my god! (Narasingha Babu enters.)
Narasingha	:	Yes, dear, once you leave the house, money moves ahead while you stay behind.
Nanu	:	What was the daily expenditure at the five-star hotel?
Suchi	:	Who knows? I have no idea. The bill must be with him. Go and ask.

Narasingha	:	What's the need? Let him take his wife wherever he wants. Why should we worry?
Suchi	:	No, Dad, he's very interested in knowing all the details.
Nanu	:	But aren't you the information officer? What information will you provide us with if you need help keeping track of even these little details? (Mother enters.)
Nirmala	:	Why are you pestering her, Nanu? Are you turning into a child day by day? (Suchi's phone rings, but she misses the call.)
Suchi	:	He must have called. (Worried) What should I do? I don't know how to call back.
Nanu	:	I would have called, but...
Suchi	:	Please make the call.
Nanu	:	No, your phone is varnished and may get scratched, and its paint may fade.
Nirmala	:	He's probably somewhere in the market. He'll be back soon. Don't worry.
Narasingha	:	Still, the call got disconnected while ringing.
Nirmala	:	That's true.
Narasingha	:	Am I acquainted with his ringtone? I thought the sound was coming from somewhere else. (Surya arrives.)
Surya	:	So, you're all here. You didn't pick up the call. Calls used to cost money in the past, but not anymore.
Suchi	:	It got disconnected as soon as I picked it up. Sorry.

Surya	:	No matter how often I explain to you that time is money (precious), you'll never give up your middle-class mentality. You say sorry in every sentence, cry and shed tears and swear your life away at everything.
Narasingha	:	Dear! Suchi will remain a child until she learns to take on responsibilities.
Suchi	:	Why don't you tell us why you called?
Surya	:	You've spoiled my mood!
Suchi	:	Sorry!
Surya	:	I had to submit a tender and make deals with many multinational companies.
Suchi	:	I understand.
Surya	:	I said I would drop you here and go home.
Nirmala	:	Son! It's okay, you work all the time. Please stay here for some days. We've been eagerly waiting to welcome you.
Surya	:	Yes, but...
Nirmala	:	You will understand us once you become a father yourself. May God bless you with a child soon. Then you'll realize your parents' heart.
Narasingha	:	Go on, kids, talk to each other. Spend time understanding each other. Learn from your experiences.
Surya	:	Nanu, do you have your mobile?
Nanu	:	Dad said, "He'll buy me a new phone when I go to Bangalore this time."
Surya	:	Nanu, come with me; I'll buy you a new one.
Narasingha	:	No, son, you've just returned from a

		long trip. You must have spent a lot. I've already seen a few models at the shop. I'll buy one for him within three to four days.
Nanu	:	Dad, as per my sun sign, the red colour would suit me. I want a red-coloured phone.
Surya	:	Does the sun sign really determine the colour? That's interesting.
Narasingha	:	Son, what's your astrological or sun sign?
Surya	:	I don't know anything about that. It's all old-fashioned. I remember my date of birth only. It's on 18 February 1976. I don't know anything else.
Nanu	:	You don't even know this much? Yet, you're the sun, the source of all energy, and your wife is the information officer herself. (Laughing romantically at his own joke)
Surya	:	I don't understand your words, Nanu.
Nanu	:	What's there to understand? You're the energy source, the Sun God himself, and your wife, my sister, is an information officer. Did you get me?
Narasingha	:	(laughing) Our Nanu has learned many things after leaving home.
Nirmala	:	Be a Roman when you are in Rome. Would he stay at home forever?
Surya	:	Nanu, do you know what the stock market is? Or the cost of an IPL match? Or at what temperature do glaciers in the Himalayas melt?

Nanu	:	But I know about my parental lineage, astrological sign, star sign, and my grandfather's name. I also know about the expenses of this house and my mother's medical expenses at the hospital.
Nirmala	:	Nanu, you've said enough.
Nanu	:	Mom!
Nirmala	:	He's the elder son-in-law. You've teased him enough. Let it go now.
Surya	:	Forget it, Mom. I didn't mind his words.
Suchi	:	Nanu, when did your 10+2 (intermediate course) results come out?
Nanu	:	I don't remember. (Surya laughs and leaves. Suchi follows, and Nanu follows him.)
Nirmala	:	Tell me, in which *Skanda* (chapter) of the Shrimad Bhagavad does Dhruva *Charita* (Character) fall?
Narasingha	:	I can't remember. Let's look it up. It could be on the sixth *Skanda*.
Nirmala	:	Okay. We need to remember many things once we stop practising.

SCENE- IV

(Archana and Suchana are sitting.)

Suchana	:	*Apa* (Sister), where is your son?
Archana	:	He went with his father. He'll be back the day after tomorrow after visiting his grandparents.
Suchana	:	Archi *Di* (to sister respectfully), you're very fortunate.

Archana	:	You've had the chance to visit many hill stations. I wonder if I'll have the same fate.
Suchana	:	(distracted) Yes, but...
Archana	:	Suchi, is this your new necklace? A gift from Surya?
Suchana	:	The one I received during the wedding was heavy and unsafe to wear outside. So, he got me a new one.
Archana	:	How much does it weigh (in grams)? How expensive is it? The price of gold has skyrocketed.
Suchana	:	I don't know.
Archana	:	What's this? I quarreled with my husband until I discovered a saree's price. That's why your brother-in-law never removes price tags; he keeps them intact.
Suchana	:	*Apa* (Sister)! There's no need for me to know anything. I am curious to know how much he earns, where he goes when he returns, or anything about his business.
Archana	:	What are you saying? (Nanu enters.)
Nanu	:	Information Officer! What's your husband's programme?
Archana	:	Go away. He's come here again to chatter. We were discussing something serious just now.
Nanu	:	What serious topic, sister? This is like a bird trapped in a gold cage. She doesn't know how much gold is used in the cage or the difference between gold and iron cages.

Suchana	:	Dad said, "An office-going son-in-law will receive his salary at the end of the month and distribute the same throughout the month, while the son-in-law, a businessman, will hand over cash daily to my daughter. She'll be tired of counting, but it won't stop. (Her voice becomes heavy.)
Nanu	:	I teased you greatly when the Right to Information Act was passed. We had an Information officer at home. You were thrilled.
Suchana	:	I thought I'd studied enough. I'd get a job somewhere and live independently.
Nanu	:	And you married into the Adhikari family. It seemed fitting.
Suchana	:	No, my dear brother, no puns work here. I can't navigate that maze. Sarees, jewelry, unrestricted shopping... We have servants and priests at our beck and call. I could get what I asked for. What more information do I need?
Archana	:	Does that mean you'll forget cause and effect, your education, and your family background?
Suchana	:	*Apa*, I've grown up doing calculations. That's why Dad trusts me more than any one of you.
Nanu	:	But in the end, all your calculations went wrong, didn't they? (Nirmala arrives.)
Nirmala	:	What are you saying?
Suchana	:	Yes, Mom, your daughter's name is Suchana, yet she knows nothing.

Nirmala	:	Everything you taught me is useless now. I don't understand these kids today. Just think about how I managed to raise you all. I worried about every little thing. I used to wonder why there was only one kernel in a mango: you all used to cry for two kernels. Now that you have everything, you're still unhappy.
Nanu	:	Suchi *Didi* (Sister), are you thinking about Mom? Don't, or else you'll go crazy.
Archana	:	Mom, Dad and you three used to look at each other while calculating.
Nirmala	:	What about the fact that my son-in-law took you on a flight? He has provided you with sarees, cars, and jewellery. You are fortunate enough to enjoy your life.
Suchana	:	Yes, your son-in-law calculated the cost of a call before my dad, and I felt ashamed that day.
Nanu	:	But I understood one point.
Archana	:	You haven't understood anything. Take care of yourself. Who will be that girl to come to this house as a bride who must have done great service to Lord Shiva?
Nanu	:	Why did you change the topic? I understood that the Right to Information Act is a mythical, scary creature or a *kokua*. It never exists in life.
Suchana	:	Why? Many people receive a lot of information. Who are we to call the mythical creature *Kokua*?
Nanu	:	Yes, information like how much my husband earns, the electricity bill, and

		the weight of the jewellery I wear will be provided by the Information officer as well. Great! (Narasingha Babu enters.)
Narasingha	:	Yes, we're unaware of many things, just like my lineage, the full name of my village, my uncle's house. We've forgotten all that, even our mother tongue. We're not ashamed of that.
Archana	:	Yet we remember the duration and cost of a local call, the stock market, email addresses, and websites—all updated daily.
Narasingha	:	People will call you outdated if you don't know these.
Nanu	:	Will you forget your astrological/ sun sign while remembering these? Where is this written, Dad?
Narasingha	:	Today, the kids are far away from their lands. To remember one's tradition is to recognize one's roots/ lineage. That day, your mother asked about Dhruva Charita. I looked it up immediately and told her. That's my stubbornness. You'll progress only if you remain stubborn.

SCENE- V

(Archana and Nanu are sitting and discussing.)

Nanu	:	*Apa* (Sister), my nephew should have been here. You're leaving the day after tomorrow, and I'll leave the day after that. I won't be able to see him anymore.
Archana	:	What can I do about that? Perhaps we can't properly take care of him in this

		house. That's why his father didn't bring him here.
Nanu	:	Your husband is lovely, Archi *Didi*. You're making up stories. (Suchana enters.)
Suchana	:	Brother, everyone seems nice from the outside. The person who's tasted the coconut knows how tender it is inside. (Nirmala enters.)
Nirmala	:	Dear Archi, I've packed *badhi* (small lumps of pounded pulses dried in the sunlight), pickles, and coconut for you. Also, cumin, chilli powder, and the best spices we have had. Should I pack flattened rice, too?
Archana	:	It's enough, Mom. The luggage will become heavy. I have to carry my son's belongings as well.
Nirmala	:	What else do you want to take?
Archana	:	Why will I long for what's not in my lot or fate?
Nirmala	:	My dear, don't say so. I will be hurt. Your parents are here for you. You have an able husband and a child. What else do you need to worry about?
Archana	:	Mom, look at our Suchi. How smart and intelligent she is! God has gifted her the ability to make her everyone in the world... But...
Nirmala	:	But what? Why did you stop?
Archana	:	Her intelligence is futile now. She's like a showcase doll that moves when her key is twisted. (Suchana enters.)

Suchana	:	Mom, do you know all my friends envy my fate? (Narasingha Babu enters.)
Narasingha	:	Nanu, what are you discussing here with the ladies?
Nanu	:	No, Dad, I was thinking about this Right to Information.
Nirmala	:	He's a thinker or philosopher.
Nanu	:	No, Dad, I can't get into or understand this Right to Information Act. All these newspapers provide information about climate change, earthquakes, and cyclones and even warn the fisherfolk community. But what's this information? Who will give it, why, and how?
Narasingha	:	You can say it, but I can't. All these prominent leaders or politicians declare information about their property to the public, but only some are legitimate. Are all the calculations made by astrologers true? No, then!
Nanu	:	Why did you talk so much, Dad? We, the middle-class people, are happy talking about the Rickshaw fare, the discount on our clothes, or from which shop we can afford to buy one and get one free offer. We're happy whether anyone else hears it or not.
Narasingha	:	Leave that. Surya Babu contacted us over the phone. He has some work. He won't be able to come to us. You'll have to drop your sister at her in-laws' house.
Nanu	:	Dad... me?
Narasingha	:	I'm asking you because you're here.

	Otherwise, I would have gone. (Softly) I didn't like what Surya said the other day. Don't say this to anyone. Your mom will be upset and hurt if she hears it.
Nanu	: I understand, Dad. I'm no longer a kid. But five years ago, I used to think that our sister was not just the information centre of our house, but she would become the information centre of the entire world. All the information will be on the tip of her tongue. Wasn't I a kid back then?
Narasingha	: O stupid fellow! I also wanted to keep the account details private from your mom. I used to think she was meddling/interfering too much in my business. Yet, because of her intelligence, we now have a building to live in.
Suchana	: Dad, what's in this bag? I have brought it from there.
Narasingha	: It has a few sarees in it. My daughters have come after a long time, so you choose them with your choice. I am leaving. (He leaves.)
Suchana	: Mom, whichever you select will be good.
Nirmala	: Archi, you're staying out of Odisha. You choose first.
Archana	: Mom, I won't select. Let Nanu choose for me.
Nanu	: I'm sitting among ladies. Have you heard of our dad now? Return all these sarees. These girls hesitate to express their choices even in front of their parents. You girls are great! Dad, these sarees could be

	better. These girls don't lack anything. Tell me which shop you got them from. I'll return them, or if you say, I'll keep one for my mom.
Nirmala	: Anger lies at the tip of his nose. Let me choose for my daughters. You should have brought a few more sarees. (To her husband)
Archana	: Suchi, what did you get for your sisters-in-law from Shimla?
Suchi	: He took it away in that bag.
Archana	: Leave it. What do we have to do with that? They're rich people.
Nanu	: Sisters, you don't know anything. I have told you rightly. The Right to Information and Information Officer are not the same; they are two different entities. The Right to Information is like a mythical, scary creature. Shrewd people create it to frighten others.
Archana	: Leave it. Suchana Adhikari (or the Information Officer) herself has visited our house.
Nanu	: Apa, you're mistaken again. Suchana is just the name of a girl, whether she is an *Adhikari* (officer), *Sadachari* (righteous), or *Bekari* (unemployed). Suchana is just a girl. She doesn't have even the simplest information. She gets hurt by her own people when she tries to realize it. (Narasingha Babu enters.)
Narasingha	: What did you say, my dear? I couldn't hear. Please repeat.

Nanu	:	No, Dad, I have just said, Suchana is just the name of a girl, that's it. When she's at home, she obeys and doesn't answer much. And the rights are all false: if you ask for them, you won't get them; you must snatch them away.
Narasingha	:	Stop saying all this. You'll go and drop your sister tomorrow.
Nanu	:	I'll go, Dad. Mom is doing all the preparation. Everything is here out of the way. Mom doesn't know. My poor mother!
Narasingha	:	Stop showing sympathy to your mother and take care of yourself. Take pride in the information you have and stand up for yourself. You'll see, everything comes on track or will be solved naturally.
Nanu	:	Now I understand. Suchana is just the name of a girl. It's her own will whether to be an Adhikari or not.

END

Last Quarter of Anticipation

Dramatis Personae

Shankar	:	An old Gandhian
Bipin	:	Shankar's son
Alert	:	Shankar's grandson
Parbati	:	Shankar's wife
Nancy	:	Shankar's foreign daughter-in-law
Alice	:	Shankar's foreign granddaughter

SCENE- I

(It's an ashram school in a rural area. An older woman is murmuring to herself in the afternoon.)

Parbati : Oh, God! Is this what is destined for my life? I can't bear it anymore. Please, take me off this world.

Shankar : (Coughing) Why are you crying, Parbati? You were born to dedicate your life to Lord Shiva's penance.

Parbati : Stop those stories. I can't bear them anymore.

Shankar : You must, even if you've grown weary of

it because I haven't learnt anything else to tell.

Parbati : You're truly cruel. I have understood that my son may be somewhere in this world, but he'll always be in God's embrace. Today, even that solace slips away. (crying) (Students call from outside.) Guruma', please come! We've rescued a baby deer!

Shankar : Parbati! See how much you're loved and revered. You are the mother of so many children; even a baby deer has come to seek share from your care.

Parbati : This is nothing new. I've been a mother to all since this orphanage opened.
Many deer, rabbits, and fawns like this have come and gone. So, are all these efforts worthwhile?

Shankar : You say, "Did I deny Banu to come to our home? He stayed away from us willingly."

Parbati : You didn't, but... you didn't exactly encourage him, either. Did you ever say, "Forget everything and bring your children back?"

Shankar : You've been with me for so long, yet you still don't understand me. How could Banu or my daughter-in-law understand me? Moreover, She's a foreigner.

Parbati : Don't forget, one day, you married me against everyone's wishes.

Shankar : You've told me this countless times. I have explained it to you, too. You have

Parbati	yet to try to understand this. Marriage, for me, was a statement for social reform.
Parbati	: Yes, social reform. (Passionately)
Shankar	: I didn't love you. I didn't send you any love letters or meet you anywhere privately.
Parbati	: (Equally passionate) I was a child widow. When I was sixteen, I was often weeping secretly at our home. I was locked inside the day when there was fish and mutton curry at my home. I was forbidden to wear, even touching colourful sarees. The khadi that I used to wear turned dirty repeatedly. I can't look at anybody eye to eye. I had to obey the strict order of my elder brother.
Shankar	: Were those days not painful?
Parbati	: Yes, the world moved on, but I remained trapped. The girl widowed was within four walls with all kinds of restrictions. If I move anywhere, many complications arise against me.
Shankar	: The workers once visited your village to campaign for Gandhi's thoughts and principles. I heard the people shouting at your home and the filthy language used against you. I stopped, not just that day, but for a lifetime. (Laughing)
Parbati	: Do you still remember all those incidents from the erstwhile days?
Shankar	: Yes, the news spread to the Panchayat. Till that time, I hadn't seen your face. But I was overpowered by irresistible thought

		and determined to save your life and to give you social prestige and dignity.
Parbati	:	You were the best of men to me. I silently agreed to your proposal before my superiors. I remembered I had many things to do. You were my saviour who pulled me out of the darkness. Ahh... where did those days go?
Shankar	:	Today, we seem tired, spiritless and dim. We are over sixty years old and live in love with our dear ones. Otherwise, how can I live strongly after so many years?
Parbati	:	I recall the orphanage children bringing you home after you collapsed. You spent five days senseless in the hospital at that time. What pride is in it? Again, this son...
Shankar	:	Parbati, you can say it, but I can't. But we have similar kinds of experiences. I married you with great pride and left my home. We embarked on a mission to save lives in this dense forest while forging our own. And what have we gained?
Parbati	:	I agreed to welcome our daughter-in-law to our home after she visited Bhubaneswar. I met her again. I explained to her about our lifestyle and coached them in our household's ways. I have yet to tell you anything about this. Despite this, she defied me. We've lost our son, now our daughter-in-law!
Shankar	:	Those two kids... What will they be doing? For the last two days, his image

	has danced before my eyes. I haven't seen him since he became a father. Did he speak of me to his son? Nobody knows!
Parbati :	How old will those kids be? Yes, they must be the same age as Banu was when he'd ask, "Mom, where is my maternal uncle's house? Why doesn't anyone visit us from your dad's house?"
Shankar :	Indeed, his kids must wonder the same.
Parbati :	I've spent my life trying to please you. I have sacrificed my happiness. Binu left us for his joy, too. How can we trust Bipin?
Shankar :	Parbati, do you still have faith in Bipin? You're, indeed, very simple and generous.
Parbati :	Why not? A male child's fate hides beneath the leaves. It changes as the leaves fly. Have patience. Don't lose your hope.
Shankar :	Don't waste time dwelling on the past. The kids will be here soon. We must prepare ourselves for them.
Parbati :	Won't their mother accompany them?
Shankar :	Stop dreaming all that. Inform the Ashram school headmaster. Let him leave for Bhubaneswar tomorrow. The flight's at four-thirty.
Parbati :	(Sighing deeply) Only God knows their fate. My grandchildren are coming, and I've never met them. I've never seen my daughter-in-law in bridal attire, nor will I. Who else lives feeling suffocated like this?
Shankar :	Don't worry or fret. We've nurtured and

	nursed many children here. They adore you. You're integral to their happiness. The Ashram School thrives because of your dedication and devotion. Isn't that an achievement? Be grateful to God for what you have instead of worrying about what you don't.
Parbati :	What you said is so true, yet useless to me. No work can be done with articles once used by someone and then picked up.
Shankar :	You remember how I once taught you English forcefully?
Parbati :	You scolded me for not being able to comprehend the meaning of the word *'mission'*. Then, after spending a sleepless night, I memorized the *Childs's Easy First Grammar* book. I wrote down the meanings of the English words. Then, I learned how to write down an application. I remember it all.
Shankar :	Would he have roamed around like this if five per cent of your determination had passed down to your son Bipin? Wouldn't he have pondered about his future? It's *the System's* fault! Can we change the *System*? See how I have remained as an *outcast* till the very end.
Parbati :	He says, if you wanted, he could have got a job. You don't wish to see his happiness.
Shankar :	I resigned as a government employee and served my nation. He is bound to despair if he hopes this from me.

Parbati	:	Leave that. Tell me, what preparations have you made for tomorrow? The kids will join us.
Shankar	:	Do we know about their likes and dislikes? Do what is appropriate.
Parbati	:	I have already asked the fishmonger to provide fresh fish. I brought milk to prepare curd as well. I will also soak pulses, especially black gram and rice. I wish to prepare a few *chakuli* (Rice pancakes) tomorrow evening.
Shankar	:	Can we do anything special after all?
Parbati	:	Forget and let go of all the past incidents. The man who we believed, our pride, had left this mundane world permanently. Again, pride will only suit us a little at this age.
Shankar	:	Yes, once the old father's able sons were the reason for his pride. Time has changed.

SCENE- II

(There was the sound of a vehicle arriving. Alert and Alice come rushing. They are fourteen and twelve years old, respectively.)

Alert	:	Good day, Grandpa! I am your grandson Alert.
Alice	:	Grandma, I am Alice.
Parbati	:	(Hugging both) You are fluent in Odia. I was afraid of how I would communicate or gossip with you two.

Alice	:	Our Daddy says, "India is the best country in the world. Odia is the most beautiful language because it is his mother tongue."
Parbati	:	Good!
Alice	:	But I can understand Odia fully.
Shankar	:	Very good, dear! It is great that your dad has taught you Odia.
Alice	:	Yes, Grandpa.
Shankar	:	Where did your mom go? Parbati, didn't you welcome our daughter-in-law inside? You seem mesmerized after seeing these two. (Nancy enters slowly and touches Shankar and Parbati's feet, greeting them. She is very calm and composed.)
Nancy	:	Baba, I am your unfortunate daughter-in-law.
Shankar	:	Dear, it is not you who is unfortunate, but we are. You have reached us now. You will now take care of everything. This house... This school...
Nancy	:	No, Dad, I have lost interest in everything.
Shankar	:	But why?
Parbati	:	(To Shankar) Can you listen to me?
Shankar	:	Parbati
Parbati	:	I can't understand what she is saying. Please explain it to me.
Shankar	:	She is not interested in staying here. Hello, my dear! Can you understand what we say?
Nancy	:	I can understand a little. After the death of Bana Bihari, I have joined a Charitable Hospital.

Shankar	:	Please think of your children, Nancy. Please give it a second thought.
Nancy	:	I know you are the right person for my children. I want to go back soon. I will leave tomorrow morning, Maa.
Parbati	:	Dear, you have visited after so long. We have yet to see you properly.
Nancy	:	I have seen your photos and heard many stories about you. You are the ideal mother. Please take care of your grandchildren.
Shankar	:	Parbati, do you remember when I scolded you for not knowing the meaning of the word 'mission'? Our Nancy has dedicated her life and promised to live with this mission. Could you not stand in her way? Let her go.
Parbati	:	Indeed, you are so cruel. The kids still need to wash themselves. They have run off somewhere. The daughter-in-law has said so in self-respect, and you're asking her to leave.
Shankar	:	Not self-respect, Parbati, understanding... realization. No one takes such a decision unless struck by the conscience. You see, Parbati, Nancy's good deed will make us proud one day.
Parbati	:	(Breathing heavily) The worry of managing kids at this age! Do you understand?
Nancy	:	Yes, Mom, you can! You can do it better than anybody else. I know.
Parbati	:	Do you have so much faith in me?

Nancy	:	Banu was saying that you are like a living Goddess.
Parbati	:	Goddess or something else? (speaking to herself). Life comes to an end if one is considered a goddess. Eyes turn to stone, the mouth is shut, and one doesn't experience sorrow or happiness. How can you?
Nancy	:	I see you in my dreams. Your smiling face resembles or is very similar to Goddess Durga.
Parbati	:	My dear, I had been unfortunate enough to witness your happiness. Yet, I promise you, I will adequately nurture your kids and make them great people.
Shankar	:	Go, Parbati, make the arrangements for the departure of the daughter-in-law. We could not see the very person for whom we mourned so much. Instead, we will be entangled in the affairs of his kids. God! Will the person endowed with responsibility be forever tied to it? Can that person never be free of the burden? (Alice and Alert enter.)
Alice	:	(Affectionately) Grandma, Daddy says you are very efficient, hardworking, and affectionate.
Parbati	:	Yes, Mom says I am a goddess, the daughter calls me very affectionate… Wow!
Alert	:	(To Shankar) I have heard from my Daddy that you are a follower of Gandhi. Plain living and high thinking are your ideal. Am I right?

Shankar	:	Wow, Alert, do you know about Gandhi?
Alert	:	I have seen his image. Having seen you, you must resemble Gandhi.
Parbati	:	Oh, my grandson! You compared Gandhi with your grandfather.
Shankar	:	Why are you upset? (Laughing at his humour). Parbati, answer honestly: how many kids in our state have as much knowledge about Gandhi as our Alert does?
Parbati	:	You don't know today's kids. They have facts of general knowledge at the tips of their tongues.
Alice	:	And Grandma, what will you feed us?
Alert	:	Grandpa… no *Jeje* (Grandpa), it's already evening.
Shankar	:	Come on, kids, let's go. Let us at least pray to God.
Nancy	:	Yes, Daddy, you shall show us the path. I thought I would bring your son to you. Sorry, I could not succeed.
Shankar	:	Have patience. What man proposes God disposes. If man could achieve anything he had wished for, why would a daughter like you have stayed far away from us?
Alert	:	Grandpa, do you know the prayer?
Shankar	:	Of course. Please be seated and sing- "Oh, merciful lord of the universe! Please receive my honest prayers. On water, land, mountains and in the sky Your beauty shines everywhere high. You bless us with great thoughts and intellect,

You illuminate us the path to righteousness..."

SCENE- III

(The postman delivers a letter.)

Shankar	:	Parbati, where did you go? Listen, Bipin has sent us a letter. He is asking for a share of my property.
Parbati	:	What property do we have? Just a few books and trunk boxes, right?
Shankar	:	He's not asking for this property. He's after the landed property.
Parbati	:	Doesn't he know we have sold everything and spent it on this school? We're left with zero savings... (Bipin reaches there after a while.)
Bipin	:	Dad, don't you have any money with you? (Sarcastically)
Shankar	:	Why are you asking like a stranger? If we live with a bit of comfort, you'll depend on others at the end of the month!
Bipin	:	What do you mean by 'comfort'?
Parbati	:	Shut up, Bipin. It is not how you can talk to your dad.
Bipin	:	No, but he said 'comfort'...
Shankar	:	By 'comfort', I mean more than three to four pairs of clothes, overspending on fish and meat apart from rice and dal... all this.
Bipin	:	Thanks, Dad! You have given a good

		definition of 'comfort'! I'll keep your words in mind. I'll tell my friends the same.
Parbati	:	Bipin, have you gone mad? You've ruined yourself in your friends' company.
Bipin	:	Mom, I'm not saying anything wrong. Haven't you ever thought we could have lived more comfortably? You could have worn different sarees or gone somewhere on vacation...
Parbati	:	I no longer have the age and strength for that. I'm tired of struggling with my circumstances, and the responsibility of Banu's kids has tied me down even more. What is respite anymore?
Bipin	:	Mom, why are you avoiding my question? Are you indeed happy with your life?
Shankar	:	Can you say who is happy in life in this world?
Bipin	:	Dad, why are you interrupting? You've burdened my mom with numerous responsibilities in the name of social reform. You've drained her like a machine, making her work in the name of social service.
Parbati	:	I say, I am happy. Is it okay now? You won't understand, Bipin. Your words are like arrows to my heart. Remember, once the goal of your life is set, chasing it becomes easier.
Bipin	:	Mom, you live by my dad's ego and prestige. Being honest throughout your life, you won't earn anything.

Shankar	:	Quit the place now. I need some peace. For my institution, for your mom...
Parbati	:	Bipin, you be quiet.
Bipin	:	Dad, I'm leaving. I knew you wouldn't be able to bear my words and presence. Throughout your life, you've spoken but have yet to learn how to bear what others say. (He leaves.)
Parbati	:	Did you hear what he said? These kids in today's world look at society so superficially.
Shankar	:	What did he say? How can he live being so reactionary?
Parbati	:	Have you ever thought we have been derailed from mainstream society?
Shankar	:	But I have never compromised in my life. I have never indulged in any illegal activity. I have not hoarded money following any wrong path. Doesn't that have any value in life?
Parbati	:	Who said it doesn't have any value? People still pledge in your name, respect you, and invite you as guests. But would it have been better if Bipin had received a job offer? It would have been solved!
Shankar	:	Tell me, what problems could have been solved? Your able son Binu is asking for a share of the property.
Parbati	:	Oh, Binu became my son when he asked for a share, but he's your son when he received first division in his M. B. A. programme? Wow, how is this father

		different from other fathers? (Alice and Alert arrived.)
Alice	:	Grandma, Alert says we have become poor.
Parbati	:	What do you mean by the word 'poor'?
Alert	:	Poor' means impoverished. We study here in Ashram School. We don't have a car or mansion...
Alice	:	We bought a new dress when we came here. That's why Alert is saying...
Parbati	:	Okay, now you go. We'll visit the town during the Christmas holidays. You can shop to your heart's content.
Alert	:	Yes, but will you take us to the café and garden like our Daddy-Mommy?
Shankar	:	Certainly! We'll eat at the café and stroll in the garden, okay, kids? (Two kids walk away, sighing loudly) Parbati, I thought nurturing these two kids into adults would be as easy as nursing our kids. But I forgot, Time has changed. It's true, Parbati, that nurturing kids is no easy task now. Simple advice will no longer be fruitful; it requires avidity, potentiality, and alertness. Something would have been possible if any parent had been here with them. Let me try; I have to arrange money somehow before the vacation.

SCENE- IV

(Evening. Alice and Alert are hearing the story from Parbati. Any story can be included here)

Parbati	:	Can we wind this up? You will listen to stories all day? Won't you study?
Alert	:	Daddy said you used to teach him only through stories. We want to listen to the stories. Please, Grandma, tell us now. We've never argued with Grandpa, I mean quarrel.
Parbati	:	Did your mom ever quarrel with your dad?
Alice	:	No, never. Whenever Daddy was annoyed, my mom cried, saying she would die.
Parbati	:	Alas! What a poor soul! She lost her paternal family and accepted her husband's family, but even that bliss she was deprived of.
Alert	:	Grandma! Let's leave that. You always cry whenever we talk about mummy. Let's change the topic. Have you ever seen Gandhi?
Parbati	:	No, I haven't. Grandpa saw him in his childhood. I was a country girl. I couldn't come to Cuttack and see Gandhi.
Alice	:	Okay, Grandma, you revere Gandhi as a divine figure. Then tell me, will anyone who worships Gandhi always be in poverty?
Parbati	:	My dear! You don't understand. In those

		days, Gandhi's words were like God's. Many gave up their land and jewellery, offering them at their feet.
Alice	:	And did they never wear that jewellery again?
Parbati	:	Not only that, but women also even burnt their expensive silk sarees.
Alert	:	What did they wear then, grandma? Did those who desired to wear sarees cry?
Shankar	:	I also burnt your grandma's saree.
Alice	:	You must have gifted her a new dress then.
Shankar	:	Smart kid; she said I must have gifted her a dress.
Alice	:	Then?
Shankar	:	I gave her two handwoven or cotton sarees.
Parbati	:	I washed and wore them. The thick sarees were hard to get dried off in the monsoon.
Alice	:	You must have cried without getting more sarees from Grandpa.
Parbati	:	Did Grandpa even see my tears? He was so engrossed in the freedom movement that he didn't visit us for four months when your Daddy was born.
Shankar	:	Time flew by.
Parbati	:	Yes, I've grown old too. I realized your grandpa was not the one who can be tied to the family. God blessed me with three kids, and I was engrossed in their responsibilities, such as their studies, treatment, smiles and tears, and quarrels.
Shankar	:	Yes, time has passed. One day, I discovered

		myself at this residential school. Some unlucky poor children awaited me there.
Alice	:	What about your children?
Shankar	:	Your Daddy was studying well. So, he went abroad and settled there. And your elder uncle was also a good student. But rich lifestyle attracted him. He didn't like our family's lifestyle. Since the day he started working, he has not come here. You see your Bipin Uncle here.
Alice	:	What about our elder uncle's family?
Parbati	:	They're good, but your elder uncle wants to keep his kids away from us and the Ashram School. That's his wish.
Alert	:	Can we go to visit them? There would be fun.
Shankar	:	Okay, we'll take you someday. It's close. We will take the bus, then the train and an auto again, or we will have to walk five miles from there on foot. (Recalling) Yes, had your dad been alive today, why would you two have also come here to see us? (Getting emotional)
Alert	:	No, Grandpa, Daddy used to speak a lot about you to such an extent you can't imagine. We thought you two must be Unique.
Parbati	:	How do you feel now? Do you like us?
Alert	:	We are satisfied, but can I ask you something?
Parbati	:	Of course, go ahead.
Alert	:	If a person is honest, can't he live comfortably?

Shankar	:	Parbati, are you listening to this? The topic is 'comfort' again. Gandhi called comfort a sin. Our son asked for it that day; today, it is your grandson. Answer him, Parbati. Tell me, have I done anything wrong?
Parbati	:	Why are you so upset hearing this? Why are you taking the kids' words to your heart? We may be unable to fit the images described by their dad to them. Our looks seemed shabby, and they wondered if all honest people needed to improve. You hurt yourself listening to them.
Shankar	:	There were many opportunities in life for corruption. The word corruption didn't exist back then. The words like 'corruption' and 'bribery' also seemed new. My mother used to say that one who used to bury a hook at someone's house was called 'bribery'. (laughing at his humour)
Parbati	:	The people of our time were very good. Nowadays, offering sweets instead of betel nuts is a common practice. No work can be done without this. There won't be any file movement.
Alert	:	Grandma, what do the words betel-offering and sweet-offering mean?
Parbati	:	Then means bribery and corruption. (Looking at Shankar Babu) Am I right? People receive bribes for every work, whether small or big. They lead life in all sorts of comfort and pleasure through that money.

Alert	:	That means corruption is good. Where's the problem with that?
Parbati	:	(angrily) What do you mean by 'corruption'? Please explain to me first.
Alert	:	Grandma!
Parbati	:	Since then, you have been chattering about corruption.
Alert	:	You have promised not to get angry. Why are you angry now?
Alice	:	Shut up, Alert. Will Grandpa and Grandma listen to you or vice versa? Remember what your mummy said?
Shankar	:	You two don't ponder over everything. I'll be eighty soon. I don't need counselling from you. (walking away)
Parbati	:	Your grandpa quickly gets annoyed as he is now an old fellow.
Alert	:	How did you tolerate him? Why didn't you run away?
Parbati	:	(Laughing) It's the time for me to leave the world permanently. But being manacled to your love and affection, I can't. How would I run away before?
Alert	:	I can't understand you.
Parbati	:	I've toiled all my life. When I was about to rest, God handed me your responsibility.
Alice	:	We won't disturb you any longer, grandma.
Parbati	:	Why will I get angry? Your dad distanced us from his self-respect and ego. Now, if I don't look after his kids, who will?
Alert	:	Grandma, please help Grandpa understand. We don't need anything. Sitting

beside him, we'll listen to his stories. We'll pray with him.

"Let all be happy and prosperous in the world,
Let nobody suffer here at all."

Parbati : Then, you've memorized it? Good boy! If you remember this much, you will be different from others. You won't lack anything. You will feel good and be happy.

Alert : How will I be different? We are kids like all others.

Parbati : No, you are not the same as others. Your father was Indian, but your mother is a foreigner. Your father is dead, and your mother has left you in our care. We two are different from others but unique as well. That's why you two are unique and special as well. You are born to take greater responsibility.

Alice : What is greater responsibility?

Parbati : Seriousness. You have to get trained to take onerous social responsibilities.

Alert : Grandma, you can speak excellent English. Wah…

Parbati : Unlike you, I am not from a country where English is the first language. I couldn't learn this from school. Your grandpa taught me. I talk to the foreigners visiting our Ashram School.

Alice : But we've learnt Odia fluently. Am I right, brother? But the kids of this Ashram School don't befriend us.

Parbati	:	They will, but only after a few days.
Alert	:	Let's go, Alice. We'll see where our grandpa went. Angry old man!
Alice	:	Don't speak like that. Now, this old lady may get angry!
Alert	:	You are right. Let's go.

SCENE- V

(It's morning- Ashram School Campus. The prayer sung by the children is heard. "Oh, merciful lord of the universe! Please receive my honest prayers." Bipin calls, standing at the school gate.)

Bipin	:	Alert, Alert… Listen to me, Alert?
Alert	:	(Rushing over there) Uncle, you called for me. I was doing prayer.
Bipin	:	Good job! Which prayer were you doing? Do you understand its meaning?
Alert	:	This world is God's creation. It's a prayer for peace and happiness, asking God to bless everyone. That's what it means, Uncle. Did I get it? Right?
Bipin	:	Yes, just as God has kept you all happy!
Alert	:	I can't get you, Uncle.
Bipin	:	Where did Dad go? Mom is stuck here. You're both stuck in this Ashram School, studying a little and getting pleased with less like caged parrots. Wow!
Alert	:	Why? But we're happy here.
Bipin	:	Yes, very good! Has your grandpa ever taken you to the market or a nice

Alert	:	restaurant to feed and buy you new clothes?
Alert	:	No, but...
Bipin	:	I know you can't say anything. Why don't they ask your mom to send foreign currency if they're incapable? Instead, she has kept you two here like kittens in a litter. And you seem satisfied with the company of Grandpa and Grandma.
Alert	:	Uncle, visit our home sometime. We'll ask Grandpa about this. I can't understand what you say.
Bipin	:	Of course, you can't. My dad may not worry about me, but he's restless for you two.
Alert	:	Uncle! Don't say that. Grandma often cries thinking of you. She refuses to eat at night.
Bipin	:	And you, little boy, become emotional and break down at her crocodile's tears?
Alert	:	They talk a lot about you doing some service or business.
Bipin	:	So what?
Alert	:	Then Grandpa gets angry, and Grandma cries. That's it.
Bipin	:	And you two?
Alert	:	Closing our eyes, we sleep. Who knows when the old couple stop their quarrel? (Sir called from inside. Alert, the prayer has ended; go to your class.)
Alert	:	I'll see you next time, Uncle. Please come to our home at least once. Grandma will be happy to see you.

Bipin	:	I can't move anywhere to please someone. You two keep the old couple happy. (Shankar comes from behind.)
Shankar	:	Oh, Bipin, you're here! Thank God! Your mom isn't feeling well. She earnestly wants your presence there.
Bipin	:	Did you know I would be here?
Shankar	:	No, I came to the school on my morning walk. It's good that I met you.
Bipin	:	I was talking to Alert.
Shankar	:	You called him during his class hours. Won't his class teacher get angry? He is my grandson. I'll be ashamed if he gets in trouble and receives his complaint.
Bipin	:	Yes, you're the only one who feels ashamed. Is anyone else as shy as you?
Shankar	:	Why are you talking to me so rudely?
Bipin	:	Yes, my words always hurt you. Have you ever thought about those two kids? Don't think that only prayer will help them grow and stand in society. They have seen life. Suppose you can't let their mother know this; show them how to live. Don't spoil their life.
Shankar	:	Has Alert asked you anything?
Bipin	:	He doesn't know how to speak yet. When he comes of my age, he will question not only you but all, "For what crime were we punished here? Why were we confined to this Ashram School?"
Shankar	:	I won't let that happen.
Bipin	:	Dad, you can't do anything! You can't save a sinking boat with prayers.

Shankar	:	So, you think my sacrifice will go in vain?
Bipin	:	No, Dad, you are getting due for your sacrifice, but what about Alice and Alert?
Shankar	:	Then, what do you want to say?
Bipin	:	You have been a great man. What have I got?
Shankar	:	Bipin!
Bipin	:	I couldn't even grow under your shadow. What about my job and financial status?
Shankar	:	Have you ever thanked God for what you have been blessed with?
Bipin	:	No, Dad, I don't recognize any god. I considered you my God, following your footsteps like the Vedic scriptures. But it was all in vain. If honesty is the other name of poverty, what's the need for that honesty? What's the need for that sacrifice?
Shankar	:	If I knew my son would question me like this, then…
Bipin	:	You wouldn't be my father, right? But your social service? Your greatness for humanity? It was okay if you never thought of us. Have you ever thought of our mom? How did she manage to live her days pleasing you in this hinterland?
Shankar	:	Do you know her better than me?
Bipin	:	If I had a sister, how would you have married her off? Didn't you become a saint for our mom?
Shankar	:	Bipin!
Bipin	:	There are no saints or heroes nowadays.

		What else would you have done? You would have waited for the day when she would have eloped with somebody and left your home?
Shankar	:	Shut up, Bipin—just shut up. (He fainted.)

(The school kids came running, saying Sir had fainted.)

SCENE- VI

[Shankar Babu is bedridden. The words of Bipin echo in his ears: "Dad, if I had a sister, how would you have married her off? You would have waited for the day when she would have left the home."] (Resounds)

Shankar	:	O! O! (groaning in pain)
Parbati	:	What happened? Why are you groaning all night?
Shankar	:	I no longer wish to live, Parbati.
Parbati	:	That day, you said, you have lived with the blessings and good wishes of others. What happened today?
Shankar	:	I can't bear it anymore, Parbati. Who says that having a long life is a blessing from God? Suffering is the other name for a long life.
Parbati	:	Can I ever outwit you in words? Respecting the Almighty, I have lived long only to lose. Why will I prolong the conversation today? (Alice and Alert rush in.)

Alert	:	Okay, Grandpa, can you write a letter to our mom? She might visit us.
Parbati	:	Why hasn't your mom written a letter to you?
Alert	:	No, but Uncle said if we write to her, she might send us foreign currency.
Shankar	:	Who will send foreign currency, dear?
Parbati	:	Ignore him and go to bed. He's talking nonsense. Don't take him seriously?
Alert	:	But grandma, I'm not making this up. Our uncle said, if our mom wanted, our education wouldn't be a problem for you. It is an excellent idea. He could start a business, and we could live better.
Parbati	:	This is what your uncle taught you that day at school. For that, only your grandpa is bedridden today.
Alice	:	I didn't see Uncle. I swear I didn't. It was only my brother talking to him.
Alert	:	You know everything—stupid girl.
Parbati	:	Dear, please be quiet for a while. Your grandpa will be upset if he hears. Don't you want him to recover soon?
Alert	:	You're right. Let Grandpa recover soon. I'll get my mom's address from Grandpa and write her a letter.

(The postman shouts "telegram, telegram" from outside.)

Alice	:	(rushing) Grandma, here's the telegram. Put your signature here.
Parbati	:	Oh Lord, whose telegram is this? May everyone be in good health.
Alert	:	Grandma, you're so afraid without even reading the telegram. Let me read it.

Alice	:	I'll read it. Could you give it to me? (taking it)
Parbati	:	(frustrated) No one else. I will. (tearing it) Your elder uncle will be visiting next week.
Alert	:	That's great news. Will they all come? Their kids, too?
Parbati	:	Who knows? Humans are unpredictable.
Alert	:	Your son is coming, right? Why aren't you happy, Grandma?
Parbati	:	(intently) Why? Your father is my son. He didn't come. He won't ever visit us in this life. Did I cry? I endured everything as if nothing happened. None of you ever asked me, "Grandma, why didn't you cry?" (her voice trembles)
Alice	:	There will be so much fun when the elder uncle arrives. We can go on outings.
Parbati	:	Come, Alice.
Alice	:	You never enjoy life.
Shankar	:	Dear Alice, what kind of fun do you want?
Alice	:	(doubtful) Grandpa, aren't you asleep? I said that as a joke. Please don't take it seriously.
Shankar	:	No, dear, there's nothing to take seriously. Okay, would you let us go if they came and asked to take me and your grandma with them?
Alice	:	You're very clever. Are you a commodity? We won't give you two to anyone. (hugging him affectionately)
Shankar	:	You don't understand. They're coming

	to claim their share of property. What property do I have left? Everything I earned in this life was sacrificed for this school. Why would they take it? And we are two old people...
Parbati :	(laughing and switching over the topic) Do you think I still have the energy to look after their kids? No, dear, I can't be a governess for the kids at this age. And if you teach their kids, they'll become rustic. We won't be of any use to them. Remember that.
Alice :	You're right, Grandma. You won't go anywhere, leaving us behind.
Shankar :	Where were you two before? Now, you have come and made us entirely worldly. You've brought our past back to us. You two are very smart, very sharp. Don't ever try to deceive us, okay?
Alert :	Shall we see? How will elder uncle trouble you with us around? Shall we?
Shankar :	Did your dad and uncle leave anything else to trouble us? Let's see what God wants from us.
Alert :	We're going to send the telegram. No one needs to come here. We'll say we're going to visit our mom.
Parbati :	How clever you are... But why would I lie? Let them come. Let your uncle come alone or with his wife... let their kids come too. I want to see if the kids born to me are competent and how educated they are!

Shankar	:	Go, Parbati, serve the food to the kids. Let them feel that they are not ignored here.
Parbati	:	I've been so excited about their visit that if I were to express it in words, it would lose its value. But if they feel neglected, I'll be helpless.
Shankar	:	I don't blame you. However, time changes so fast that the ruler we used to measure time must be revised. The kids will no longer desire us. We must make ourselves desirable to them. We have to change ourselves. Parbati, tell me honestly, has all my devotion and sacrifice been in vain? Didn't you get your desired house? Desired family?
Parbati	:	You know the answer to all these questions. Please don't hurt me by asking them. The days ahead are to be lived for each other. We can only try but can't do anything.

SCENE- VII

(It's 10.00 am. Bipin comes shouting.)

Bipin	:	Alice, Alert, where did you both go?
Parbati	:	They hurried through breakfast to make it to school on time. Do you need anything?
Bipin	:	No, I just dropped in. I wanted to see the kids.
Parbati	:	Bipin, I had high hopes for you. You were my beloved son. I envisioned you as my pillar of support.

Bipin	:	Mom, mere aspirations won't suffice. Success demands hard work. Merely carrying certificates won't guarantee it. A word from Dad could have changed my life, yet neither of you tried. Instead, you focused on my mistakes.
Parbati	:	Where are you staying, dear? Come, have something to eat. Your dad isn't home.
Bipin	:	No, mom. I intend to avoid sneaking a meal in Dad's absence. I'll return when I muster the courage to face him. I heard Binu *Bhai* (elder brother) is coming.
Parbati	:	Yes, he sent a telegram.
Bipin	:	I considered consulting him and moving to Madras after that. It is better to be away from home than to be in other's prying (inquisitive) eyes.
Parbati	:	I am helpless. I can only shed tears for you! It's your decision.
Bipin	:	Don't dishearten me by saying so, Mom. Have you indeed taken for granted my dad's empty ideals? Haven't you yearned for a life of your choice? Haven't you felt inferior to others?
Parbati	:	He's struggled alone throughout his whole life, fighting against social oddities. Now he's wearied. You all should support him. Instead, you find faults in him.

(Alice and Alert get ready for school)

Alice	:	Uncle, we're ready to go to school. Grandma, it's nice to see you with your youngest son. Cook something special for him. We'll be back later. Bye…bye…

Bipin	:	I no longer have the appetite for your grandma's cooking. I need to remember the taste of homely food recipes.
Parbati	:	It's my fate, not yours. I'm thirsty, standing inside water reservoirs. Amidst the thousand salutations of *Guru Maa*, I earnestly long for your call.
Bipin	:	And dad?
Parbati	:	You're not a father yet. How can you understand a father's state of mind?
Bipin	:	I've failed as a son, so I'm a wanderer. Am I destined to be a father?

(Shankar Babu enters.)

Shankar	:	Who is inside? Oh, Bipin? Come. Sit here, let's talk.
Bipin	:	Dad, we have no common subject to discuss. (laughing sarcastically)
Shankar	:	Binu telegrammed us to come. He wants a share of the property. Could you make him understand?
Bipin	:	I have heard this before. He's your son. He is legally correct to ask for a share. What's there to discuss?
Shankar	:	What property do I have? Explain to him. Tell him to give up his childish obstinacy.
Bipin	:	Can one forsake one's inheritance simply because he lacks nothing? Will it be fair?
Parbati	:	I'll talk to him if you don't explain our situation.
Bipin	:	What about the donations from different organizations to the school?
Parbati	:	Do you also believe that we're hiding wealth?

Bipin	:	It's like a narrow lane to the blind. What's the issue?
Parbati	:	Your dad can't travel to the city for a scan. As per the doctor's prescription, he needs another ECG.
Shankar	:	Could my son take a share of this diseased heart instead? He would know how this heart weakened, repressing all dissatisfactions and annoyance.
Parbati	:	Your son can't understand you. He is neither capable nor interested. Shut up.
Shankar	:	Parbati!
Parbati	:	But I need your heart. I can't share it.
Shankar	:	You're making me laugh. This heart is only for you. How will they benefit from it? Parbati, I know my heart won't be useful to anyone except you. You, be sure.
Parbati	:	Bipin, what do you want? Why are you so rebellious?
Bipin	:	Please, you both respond to me, "Do you have to be honest to be poor? Will society respect or pity honesty? Will society reward the honest person, or will he be debarred from the mainstream of society? Can an honest man's name be pronounced in respect or pity? Please tell me, Dad. Had you been with a sister, … speak the truth. No…no… (Shankar Babu collapses)
Parbati	:	Bipin, why are you silent? Get hold of him and call a doctor immediately!
Bipin	:	It's his cunning. Whenever he talks to me, he faints. I'll be blamed. I know this.

Parbati	:	Bipin, he needs to live for Alice and Alert at least for eight to ten years. (Her voice becomes heavier.)
Bipin	:	Yes, those who survive for others seem childish and futile. How am I alive? Alice and Alert have also lived here without their parents when they are children. If Dad lives, what issue will be solved?
Parbati	:	Okay, let me see. I will request the school headmaster to phone a doctor. (She leaves.)
Bipin	:	Mom, I am also unfortunate. All say, the person whose parents are like your parents is the richest in the world. I am trying to understand why I am unsatisfied or what I have more. Have I got anything costly for others? Mom, I'm trapped in my father's shadow, unable to embrace or reject his ideals. Now you understand. You call the doctor, Mom. I'm leaving. (He leaves.)

SCENE- VIII

(It's evening. The kids are studying)

Alert	:	Grandpa, how do you feel now? Can you teach us Geography?
Shankar	:	Yes, of course, bring the Atlas.
Alice	:	Take this, Grandpa. Here are your glasses, Grandpa.
Shankar	:	(speaking slowly) The picture is our India. It's not just land, water, mountains, and hills; it's a living India. She is everybody's

mother. She breathes, smiles, cries, and even scolds. (Getting emotional) Yes, she cares for everyone; she's the mother to all...

Alice	:	Grandpa, what happened? (Caressing) Grandma, be quick. Please see, Grandpa is talking non-stop.
Parbati	:	He's old now. Let him rest. Don't disturb him.
Alert	:	Grandma! Don't get angry. Can I ask you a question?
Parbati	:	Go ahead. Why are you justifying yourself?
Alert	:	A student often comes to me. He comes to school in various cars. Do you understand?
Parbati	:	What will I understand more from this? He must be your friend.
Alert	:	His lunchbox is always filled in with biryani or Chow Mein. He never brought these before! Now he does. He also brings lots of sweets and cakes. I only know some of the names. They're delicious.
Parbati	:	Go on, what else do you want to say?
Alert	:	No, Grandma, my friend says his father is wealthy. They have black money. What does black money mean, Grandma?
Parbati	:	The wealth hoarded or accumulated in an account can't be accounted for.
Alice	:	Maybe that person doesn't know how to calculate wealth as you do?
Shankar	:	Parbati, explaining black money to these kids won't be easy. Please, stay quiet.

Alert	:	You should rest. Why do you pretend to be angry? If you don't want to explain, It's all right. But if you don't know, then I'm sorry.
Shankar	:	You two want to ride in those cars and eat that lunch.
Alert	:	Of course, yes, I want that. As earlier, we used to live with our Daddy and Mummy. Very fantastic!
Shankar	:	Black money is not at all good. (sarcastically)
Alice	:	Grandpa, you get angry over trifles. Brother didn't even mention black money. Let me explain to you – you struggled so much for independence. Why can't you at least live a little happily now?
Alert	:	Yes, all your life, you toiled in the name of ideals, and those earning black money live an easy and comfortable life.
Alice	:	Why will you stay as an outcast?
Alert	:	Yes, far from the mainstream. No one will stay as being your own. Did you see it? Even your sons abandoned you. Is being good equivalent to being poor? Grandpa, answer me if the money that can't be accounted for is black. Then is living a calculated life like Grandma's, who keeps even the most minor accounts, the life?
Shankar	:	Why are you two questioning me like lawyers? Do you wonder so much about us?
Parbati	:	Answer the kids. Don't appease them. Let them know your capacity. The same

		power that once drove away the Britishers has faded and is futile in front of your people.
Alice	:	You mean your strength...
Shankar	:	Yes, now my strength has become my weakness.
Parbati	:	Stop, don't become emotional now. (Caressing him)
Shankar	:	Parbati, I don't know whether you even recognize me. How did these kids figure me out so quickly and so soon? (Bipin enters.)
Bipin	:	Mom, may I talk to the kids today?
Parbati	:	Who said 'no' to you? Do you need anyone's permission to talk to your nephew and niece?
Bipin	:	No, but I might again influence your grandchildren. Their grandpa might feel ashamed in front of their teachers because of me.
Shankar	:	Okay, go ahead, say whatever's on your mind. Shoot as many arrows into this poor, sick father's heart as you have. But your arrows are very poisonous.
Bipin	:	I won't say anything to them, Dad; I'll tell them a story. I came specifically for that.
Alert/Alice	:	Uncle, please tell.
Bipin	:	Okay, sit and listen to me. Today, I read a story where an honest retired officer couldn't marry off his daughter. The roof of his old house had blown away.
Alice	:	Why?
Bipin	:	Her father couldn't repair the old house,

		so her uncles/ her dad's brothers divided the landed property among themselves. His share was no less. His wayward son turned too obedient to political parties for help. And the saddest part was that the dad couldn't even afford medicine for himself.
Alert	:	Then?
Parbati	:	Yes, he regretted why he was not too smart with his profession and didn't save anything for himself. His wife and children called him inefficient. His friends mocked him.
Parbati	:	Okay, I understand your story. But Alert, you can write a better story than this.
Alice	:	Grandma, I'll write the story. It will be published in our school magazine. The deadline is coming up soon.
Shankar	:	Bring the pen and paper, and I'll dictate. "An honest person lived alone in his way. He died differently from others."
Alice	:	Grandpa, wait, what does 'freedom' mean?
Shankar	:	Freedom means an exception. They laughed at him all his life; now, let them learn to respect him. Because the dead don't entertain any mockery or pride. They don't entertain... (He becomes speechless.)
Alice	:	Grandpa, please dictate slowly. I can't write so fast.
Shankar	:	(silent)
Alice	:	Grandpa, can't you hear? Won't you

		dictate the story?
Parbati	:	(Being frightened) Did he faint again or what? Anybody can call the doctor. (To herself) The doctor instructed me not to hurt him using rough language. Oh Lord, what should I do now? Let no mother suffer this fate.
Alice	:	(Caressing her grandpa) Grandpa, I don't need to write this story anymore. Please wake up. Please speak to us. Scold us, but don't stay silent.
Parbati	:	My dear, go and tell the headmaster and ask him to take his scooter and call the doctor. Fainting so many times is not a good sign for his health.
Alert	:	I'll go by cycle to the doctor.
Parbati	:	Dear, stay here with me.
Alert	:	But I'm grown up.
Parbati	:	Yes, you have grown up. Now, all the responsibilities shall be yours. But for now, stay with me. Don't go anywhere.

SCENE- IX

(Shankar Babu is lying on his bed. There is a vast crowd. Everyone has come to see him.)

Parbati	:	Kids, please be quiet for a moment. He is resting. Listen to me now; please calm down. (Bipin enters.)
Bipin	:	Mom, isn't my brother arriving today?

Parbati	:	Let him come. He'll see his father.
Bipin	:	Mom, he's not coming to see Dad. He's coming to ask for his share. He'll buy land and build a house. He'll sell this land. This uncultivated land won't be of any use to his family.
Shankar	:	(shocked) Parbati, what do you say? Have I done anything wrong? I may not listen to others, but I'll listen to you. Tell me, what's my fault?
Parbati	:	Just be quiet and rest. We'll talk about it later.
Shankar	:	I only have a little time left. I burdened you with responsibilities all my life. I never thought you could handle it. Even today, I hand over the responsibility of my school to you.
Parbati	:	You're selfish. Your son is alive. Give him the responsibility. He'll succeed.
Shankar	:	Parbati, I know, or else, why would he ask me about the school funds?
Bipin	:	Mom, stop this. Let Dad do what he thinks is right.
Parbati	:	Today, I won't be silent. I'll ask Binu to stay here permanently when he comes.
Bipin	:	Yes, let him take the responsibility here. Now that he has to take responsibility, he's recalling his son... honestly...
Parbati	:	Say whatever you want to me, but please go outside.
Bipin	:	He's old. It will happen time and again. Who else can you cast out of the house except me?

Alice	:	Uncle, you're very selfish.
Alert	:	Uncle, is he your dad?
Bipin	:	That's why I raise these points with pride. No one could understand me. Why would you?
Alert	:	Who did you understand, uncle?
Shankar	:	(Being disturbed) Parbati, sit next to me, call Banu.
Parbati	:	(worriedly) Where is Banu? Why do you behave like a lunatic? First, he deceived us all.
Shankar	:	Banu isn't here. Where did he go? Banu... Banu...
Parbati	:	He passed away in a car accident. Didn't you know?
Shankar	:	What about Binu?
Parbati	:	Binu is on his way. He'll reach soon. He'll take you to the doctor and nurse you.
Bipin	:	Yes, Binu will take good care of you.
Alert	:	Grandma, please explain to Grandpa that we won't trouble him. We'll listen to him.
Parbati	:	(to Alice) Dear, see if any vehicle has arrived.
Alice	:	(Running off and then coming back) No, no one has come.
Parbati	:	You can hear, can't you? Look carefully; Binu is coming. Bipin will stay with him. The two brothers will divide your work and lighten your burden. You'll rest on the verandah. The gardener is tired of looking at his flower-filled garden like that.
Alert	:	Grandma, what will you do?
Parbati	:	I will scold you. Study and behave. And

		I will tell your aunt to bring two cups of tea here. We are sitting here.
Alert	:	Nice, Grandma!
Parbati	:	Your uncle will fulfil all your needs. You all will live a comfortable life.
Alert	:	Grandma! Don't talk about comfort anymore. "Comfort is dangerous." Grandpa has explained this to us. We will be obedient to you. We won't trouble anyone. "Vaishnav Jana to tene kahiye" is a prayer we remember. (Humming)
Parbati	:	The Doctor has not reached us.
Bipin	:	Let me call him. Dad staying alive is extremely important to me, or else who will I ask, "Is being honest equivalent to being poor?" (He leaves.)
Parbati	:	You can ask whom you want.
Alert	:	Let me check; I can hear a car. (He leaves.)
Alice	:	Yes, two vehicles have arrived. I'll see. (She leaves.)
Parbati	:	Two? Who came? (Shankar Babu trembles.) Look, people have come in two cars. If you don't talk to them, what will I do? Could you wake up and look at me? (after a while) Okay, Binu is your son; he will wait. What about the others?
Bipin	:	(Coming back) Mom, Binu and his wife have reached. The doctor has come as well. The doctor has instructed me to take Dad to the hospital. From a far-off place, monitoring the patient will be challenging. Let's take Dad to the hospital first.
Parbati	:	Bipin, I don't think taking your dad

		anywhere is necessary. Dad has freed you all from all responsibilities. Dad will no longer be able to answer your difficult questions with a deep sigh.
Bipin	:	Mom! (crying)
Parbati	:	Son, why are you crying now? Never did you ask about how your dad was living. If anyone among us stays lonely even while surrounded by us, what pain must he suffer? No one recognized his determination and saintliness. Everyone mocked him. Leave it; why do you discuss it anymore? (Changing the tone) Call the doctor. Let him say which hospital this patient should go to. Where can he be treated properly?
Alice/Alert	:	Grandma, why are you saying this?
Parbati	:	(Firmly) Till date, everyone spoke, and I heard. Let me talk about today. I lived a whole life with this lonely man. I have provided a lot to all these kids with these two hands. The kids of my Ashram School may be in any corner of this world, but the sound of *Guruma* will always resonate in their voices. I cannot tolerate it anymore. Binu, where did you stop? Hurry up. I cannot wait any longer. Come, my dear, look at him once.
Alice	:	Grandma! Don't talk too much. The doctor must be arriving.
Parbati	:	No, dear. Who will listen to me if I shout? We can only wait until the last quarter of life.

Alert	:	Grandma, you are great, you are great.
Parbati	:	You two kids, please sing a song. My heart wants to listen to you. I am singing. You sing after me, "Oh, Lord of the universe!"
Alice	:	Grandma, sing! Why did you stop?
Alert	:	Grandma!
Parbati	:	I am leaving, kids. Be good people in life. God bless you!

END

Black Eagle Books

www.blackeaglebooks.org
info@blackeaglebooks.org

Black Eagle Books, an independent publisher, was founded as a nonprofit organization in April, 2019. It is our mission to connect and engage the Indian diaspora and the world at large with the best of works of world literature published on a collaborative platform, with special emphasis on foregrounding Contemporary Classics and New Writing.

www.ingramcontent.com/pod-product-compliance
Lightning Source LLC
Chambersburg PA
CBHW060614080526

44585CB00013B/819